FOR EVER

FOR EVER

I ALWAYS THINK IT'S FOREVER

I ALWAYS THINK IT'S FOREVER

A LOVE STORY SET in PARIS as TOLD BY AN UNRELIABLE but EARNEST =NARRATOR=

TIMOTHY GOODMAN

Simon Element

NEW YORK LONDON TORONTO SYDNEY NEW DELHI

SIMON
ELEMENT

THE STORIES IN THIS BOOK REFLECT THE AUTHOR'S (ME!) RECOLLECTION OF EVENTS. SOME OF THE NAMES AND IDENTIFYING CHARACTERISTICS HAVE BEEN CHANGED TO PROTECT THEIR PRIVACY. DIALOGUE HAS BEEN RE-CREATED FROM MEMORY, WHICH IS TOTALLY UNRELIABLE.

An Imprint of Simon & Schuster, Inc.
1230 Avenue of the Americas
New York, NY 10020

First Simon Element hardcover edition January 2023

SIMON ELEMENT is a trademark of Simon & Schuster, Inc.

For information about special discounts for bulk purchases, please contact Simon & Schuster Special Sales at 1-866-506-1949 or business@simonandschuster.com.

The Simon & Schuster Speakers Bureau can bring authors to your live event. For more information or to book an event, contact the Simon & Schuster Speakers Bureau at 1-866-248-3049 or visit our website at www.simonspeakers.com.

Book design and original artwork by Timothy Goodman

Manufactured in China

1 3 5 7 9 10 8 6 4 2

Library of Congress Cataloging-in-Publication Data

ISBN 978-1-6680-0369-5
ISBN 978-1-6680-0370-1 (ebook)

THIS IS FOR THE LONELY PEOPLE

PART 1
PARIS, FRANCE. SUMMER

PART 2
ROME, ITALY. NEW YEAR'S

Introduction
FOREVER, AGAIN

On June 31, 2019, at 8:05 PM, I took off for Paris, France, on Delta flight 264 to do something I'd never experienced before. It was the first time in my adult life I took real time off from my life. I finally did something big for myself—not for my career, not for someone else, not for some impossible facade I could never keep up with because of fear. First, a little Timothy history here: The previous year, I experienced one of my worst years, full of depression and tears. It seems I had been stalling the trauma I never worked on after all the years. It just became way too much to bear. Slowly, through therapy, I discovered that I'm worth everything, every cent I have, I was determined to make sense of my hard times and feel worthy again. Once I did, I vowed to do everything I had put off before: celebrate New Year's, grow my hair, learn French, go to Paris for six months, continue therapy, have a big birthday party, and accept real vulnerability. And while I was there, I met someone—someone who made me smile, someone who made me hit send on my heart's biggest file. Maybe it was how much my heart would eventually hurt, maybe it was the wine I drank in Parc des Buttes-Chaumont, maybe it was riding bikes in Bordeaux under the sun, or maybe it was the lonely nights after the breakup that I got drunk, but everything about Paris is forever indented on my heart.

While I was there, I learned about this unique French word called "dépaysement." It literally translates to "decountrification" or "change of scenery," but it's used to describe this great feeling of living as a stranger somewhere far away from your memory; a sort of disorientation, lost and searching, but doing it with real curiosity and wonder. That was me in Paris. Me, feeling as if I had no past or future. Me, learning the French language (while I kicked and screamed with my tutor). Me, eating all the baguettes. Me, feeling like I was meant to be exactly where I was. Me, finding someone who would turn "me" into "us." And after our love eventually dried up, after the heartbreak and fuss, after the last text I never sent sat in my notes folder collecting dust, I sit here thankful for the dust I kicked up: the good, the bad, the healing, the trauma, the boring mundane stuff that fills 99% of my life up. I believe that going after love is real as fuck, so I wanted to tell this story by writing a book.

Making art out of my own heartache doesn't feel beautiful at the time. It's not like the movies. I can't perform some grand act of self–love, discover something remarkable, and figure it all out. No, my guts are inside out. On the floor. In public. And it never seems to stop. I think: if only I do this, if only I say that, if only I hit send on that thoughtful email, then maybe it would all make sense. Sometimes I felt like I was writing this story to write us back together. Sometimes I felt like I was writing this story to write us "right" on paper. The wishful thinking, thinking my actions would matter, thinking they may reconsider . . . but they never will, dear reader. I used to think it was a curse to feel so deeply, I used to curse at myself and anyone who hurt me. Now I know it's my biggest blessing, to actually really care and fight for something. And what I've learned is how to tell my story, to remember that I'm more than someone else's memory. I've learned about the kind of partner I actually need, about the kind of partner I need to be, and that I should always be striving to see and be seen. I hope this book can give you wings for your own voyage. Healing is never linear, and as I continue my own process, I hope this book can help you feel seen. Like Donald Glover once said, "Make it all for everybody, always. Everybody can't turn around and tell everybody, everybody already knows, I told them." To own my pain, what a beautiful choice.

'SEX and THE CITY' ONCE PROCLAIMED THAT YOU ONLY GET TWO GREAT LOVES in YOUR LIFE.

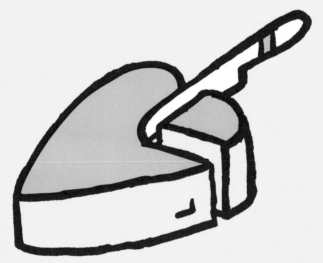

I'VE HAD FOUR.
DOES THAT MEAN I'M
LUCKY OR DOOMED?

I THINK GREAT LOVES SHOULD BE COUNTED THE WAY THE BASKETBALL HALL of FAME INDUCTS THEIR NOMINEES: A PLAYER MUST BE FULLY RETIRED FOR at LEAST FOUR FULL SEASONS. SO YOU SEE, THERE'S NO WAY AIMÉE can BE COUNTED AS a GREAT LOVE. IT JUST HASN'T BEEN THAT LONG.

YES, I WROTE Q
WHOLE BOOK ABOUT
OUR RELATIONSHIP

PAR

PARIS, FRA

RT1

CE. SUMMER

CHAPTER 1

ATTRACTION

I don't smoke, but I asked her for a cigarette. She said she didn't smoke either, but she was smoking to forget her regrets. I said I know all about that, and I asked her if I could help. She laughed and said "You must be American with a line like that!" She was wearing all denim everything, and damn, she had everything. She made me forget every piece of art I ever made. She made me wanna be a bad man just to spite my last name. I said "Je m'appelle Timothy." She said "Enchanté Timothé mon cheri, my name is Aimée. Why don't you come with me and let me buy you a drink?" and she walked back inside the party like a fuckin' G. My whole life flashed in front of me. All of my memories from that moment are tinted in purple, blue, and neon green. See, I'm a Cancer Sun and Scorpio Moon, which means that I romanticize, commemorate, and sentimen- talize every single thing. As an artist, I have to feel what I'm feeling in order to feel alive, and I felt that tingly feeling I hadn't felt since I was a teen. I looked out at the streetlights, smiled, and went back inside to follow my dreams. Two hours later, she walked me to chez moi, and Donnie & Joe Emerson's "Baby" was playing from the sky above. She looked at me and said, "Baby, you are dépaysement." I said with a grin, "Excusez-moi?" She said, "Not too bad for a Good Man." I can see her skin bleed a wisdom I've never seen, some kind of experience deeper than anyone I'd ever met in NYC. I had to wonder if it was all some sort of fantasy, some kind of idea I created during a late-night flight while eating another can of Pringles without a fight. I swear I left all my regrets back in those hotel sheets. I swear I'll stop looking at my ex's Instagram for at least a week. Was I dreaming like Tom Cruise in *Vanilla Sky*? I just know I'd never felt this alive, totally free of any conspiracy or time. When I went inside, I immediately looked that word up, called her, and we talked all night.

EVERY TIME I FALL IN, LOVE IT'S SUMMER

GETTING READY for PARIS

01 LEARN FRENCH

CLASS + DUOLINGO

02 BOOK FLIGHT

S/O DELTA!

03 BOOK AIRBNB

5TH ARR.

04 CANCEL -your- INTERNET

SAVE MONEY

05 FORGET about your GLUTEN ALLERGY

HOT BAGUETTES

06 THROW a PARTY

"AU REVOIR!"

07 FINISH -your- WORK

"OUT OF OFFICE"

08 FIND TUTOR

WWW.COM

09 EAT at your FAVE SPOT

"TU ME MANQUE"

JULY 1

WELL, I MADE IT ON THIS FLIGHT TO PARIS. AND I AM EXCITED TO START A JOURNAL AGAIN. I WAS ALWAYS JEALOUS OF THE KIDS WHO WERE IN STUDY ABROAD PROGRAMS IN COLLEGE, BUT SINCE I WAS BROKE, I WAS NEVER ABLE TO DO IT. I'VE BEEN PLANNING THIS VOYAGE FOR 3 MONTHS, INCLUDING LEARNING FRENCH (WHICH IS TRÉS DIFFICILE). I JUST WANT TO BE SCARED AGAIN! LAST YEAR, I WENT THROUGH SO MUCH DEPRESSION, AND LIFE AND WORK GETS TO A POINT WHERE I CAN'T FIND THE SPECTACULAR IN THE ORDINARY LIKE I ONCE DID. IT'S A PRIVILEGE MOST FOLKS, INCLUDING MUCH OF MY FAMILY, COULD NEVER EXPERIENCE. I WILL NOT TAKE IT FOR GRANTED. IMMERSING MYSELF IN A NEW COUNTRY WITH A DIFFERENT LANGUAGE AND CULTURE IS SCARYYYYY. AND EXCITING! AND ROMANTIC! AND SOMETHING TO TELL MY GRANDKIDS ABOUT! I MEAN, IT'S PARIS! BEING AN ARTIST IN PARIS WAS MY SECOND DREAM AFTER BEING AN ARTIST IN NYC. SOMETIMES YOU GOTTA FREE YOURSELF FROM WHAT YOU KNOW IN ORDER TO SEE YOURSELF MORE CLEARLY.

"D" WORDS

As I was running late to meet Aimée, that French word "dépaysement" kept running through my head over and over again. It reminded me that there are so many "D" words to worry about in the beginning of a relationship. Like when my friends tell me not to appear "desperate" or act like a "dick" or a "douche." I'm also reminded that I should not be in "denial" about dating, and that I shouldn't be "dramatic" about how much I like them, nor give any "disclaimers" about what I want, or get too "deep" too soon because I wouldn't want anyone to think I was too "dark." (*Donnie Darko*, oh please no!) But out of all these "D" words, the only word I'm really concerned with is an "F" word called "flirting." When you really like someone, this "F" word is scarier than all the other "F" words like "failure" or "fake" or "faithless" or "ferocious" or "Frankenstein" or "face-less" or "Fox News." Am I being too "forward?" Am I being too "formal?" Instead of going with the "flow," I just internally "freak" out as I try not to come off like some fake, douche dickhead who ferociously watches Fox News. So, as I arrived at the park to meet her for our, ahem, "FIRST" "DATE" (what a perfect combination of "D" and "F" words!), I decided that I'll live by the "D" word I love most called "Danger" and I'll happily die by the most dangerous of all the "F" words called "Feelings." After all, I am in "France!"

HOW DID YOU MEET?

"SHE & I MET DURING PRIDE WEEKEND in NYC at AN EVENT ON THE ROOFTOP. WE HIT it OFF & SPENT 15 HOURS STRAIGHT TOGETHER, WALKING AROUND THE CITY UNTIL 7 in THE MORNING."

"I MET HIM at A PARTY and OUR FIRST CONVO WAS A PHILOSOPHICAL DEBATE ABOUT KANYE. I REMEMBER LOOKING AT HIM and FEELING FOR THE FIRST TIME IN A WHILE that I WAS HOME."

"WE MET at WORK. I FOUND OUT I WAS PREGNANT with MY EX'S BABY. HE ENDED UP WAITING for ME."

"WE MET on MATCH.COM. I PAID FOR 6 MONTHS UP FRONT & HE MESSAGED ME RIGHT AWAY. I TELL HIM ALL the TIME HE was WORTH ALL $140."

"I SAW HIM in A BAR IN BROOKLYN. HE was SHY SO I INTRODUCED MYSELF. IT TURNS out WE WENT to the SAME HIGH SCHOOL. SAME YEAR TOO. WE GOT MARRIED 4 YEARS LATER."

"WE SAT NEXT to EACH OTHER on A 5-HOUR FLIGHT. 30 YEARS LATER, a BEAUTIFUL DAUGHTER, ALONG WITH CANCER and TWO HEART ATTACKS but STILL GOING STRONG."

"THE FIRST TIME WE MET I WAS GETTING a TOUR AROUND MY NEW OFFICE for MY NEW JOB. HE WAS in THE BREAK ROOM HYSTERICALLY CRYING BE-CAUSE his DOG WAS GETTING PUT DOWN THAT DAY. WE'VE BEEN TOGETHER SINCE."

"I WAS IN THE 4TH GRADE, SHE WAS IN THE 5TH. I WAS BEING CHASED BY SOME 5TH GRADE BULLIES. SHE STEPPED in & STOPPED THEM."

"MY WIFE and I MET AT a SWING DANCING CLASS in COLLEGE! SHE WAS the MOST BEAUTIFUL WOMAN in THE WORLD."

CHAPTER 2
ROMANCE

She looked at me and said, "My family is my biggest weakness, not my strength," and I felt a fire inside of me because never more could I relate. Forty minutes into our first official date, not only did I feel weak about Aimée's strength, but I also felt like I had already known her for weeks. She had on a long black dress as we drank coffee in the park, the Chuck Taylors she had on got all dirty when she beat me in pétanque. She had one of the all-time greatest laughs, when she laughed she laughed with real sincerity, and that made me feel very close to her, emotionally. As coffee became dinner, she told me to order in French with the waiter. So, we drank and ate until it got way too late, and I asked myself if this could be fate. I asked her if she ever felt the weight of life so much that she wanted to escape. She laughed and said, "No, babe, I'm a Libra, so every night I sleep great." Some people can make me question whether I was born in the wrong century. Some people make me wonder if I was born to the wrong family, in the wrong city, that maybe I

can actually be whoever I wanna be, that maybe
a life ain't a life until there's someone there to
share it with me. I knew my past was somewhere
tied up on a leash. I knew time wasn't short, so
I had to stop longing for the past all the time. So,
I was determined to be on time for love just as
urgently as the French protest in the streets. While
we shared a scooter down the winding Parisian
streets, she started singing "Singin' in the Rain"
when it started to rain, but she sang it in French
as I videoed the whole thing. I knew then that I
was falling for her because when you're falling
for someone, you really try to listen to everything
they say because everything they say says some–
thing about who they are. Our day became the
night, and then came the morning light. The sun
poked its head from behind the dusty dawning.
My head was heavy, but my mind wasn't close to
yawning. I was beyond smitten. I felt my heart's
story being rewritten. I saw the vision of our
future children. I knew I had to see her again
and again and again.

YOU KNOW YOU
REALLY LIKE SOME
ONE WHEN YOU
REALLY TRY TO
LISTEN TO EVERY
THING THEY SAY
BECAUSE EVERY
THING SAYS SOME
THING ABOUT
WHO THEY ARE

20 FIRST Dates

40-120
SHARED DRINKS

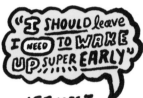

15 TIMES I
SAID THIS

14 TIMES
I WORE THE
SAME OUTFIT

12 TIMES I
EXPLAINED WHY
'THE FAMILY STONE'
IS THE BEST XMAS
MOVIE EVER

20 TIMES I
HAD TO SAY WHAT
I DO, WHERE I
GREW UP AND HOW
I STILL WANT
TO GO TO JAPAN

20 TIMES I
EXPLAINED WHY
I DON'T LIKE
STRAWBERRIES

20 TIMES I
REMEMBERED
TO NOT USE
MY PHONE
(IT'S NOT POLITE)

20 TIMES I
DESPERATELY
TRIED NOT TO
EAT HOW I
ALWAYS EAT

16 TIMES I
HAD TO TELL THEM
I NEVER SAW
MAD MEN, THE WIRE
OR GAME OF THRONES

JULY 12

WAIT, THERE ARE BREAD LAWS IN FRANCE?! I CAN'T BELIEVE I DIDN'T KNOW THIS. THE LAW STATES THAT BAGUETTES HAVE TO BE MADE ON THE PREMISES WHERE THEY'RE SOLD AND CAN ONLY BE MADE WITH FOUR INGREDIENTS: WHEAT FLOUR, WATER, SALT, AND YEAST. THEY CAN'T BE FROZEN AT ANY STAGE OR CONTAIN ADDITIVES OR PRESERVATIVES, WHICH ALSO MEANS THEY GO STALE WITHIN 24 HOURS. THIS IS WHY THEY TASTE SO INCREDIBLE! I LITERALLY EAT ONE BAGUETTE A DAY BY MYSELF...T'INQUIÈTE PAS! IN OTHER NEWS, I MET SOMEONE WHO I REALLY LIKE. AND IT'S EXCITING TO BE EXCITED ABOUT SOMEONE! I FEEL A LITTLE NERVOUS BECAUSE IT'S BEEN AWHILE SINCE I'VE FELT THIS WAY. I HAVE SOME FEAR OF BEING HURT OR DISAPPOINTED BECAUSE BREAKUPS TAKE A BIG TOLL ON ME, BUT I DON'T WANNA RUN AWAY OR WATER DOWN MY FEELINGS ANYMORE. ALSO, I'M SO HAPPY I DECIDED TO STAY IN THE 5TH (5ème).

THE COFFEE DATE

"Hey you wanna get coffee?" is historically the quintessential quasi, "this isn't a date, but it kinda is, but it doesn't have to be, but it could turn into a date if we really like each other enough to continue this caffeinated chitchat after the unwritten *I can easily bail after 30 minutes because we only made plans for coffee* rule, where we'll decide if we like each other enough to potentially turn this coffee hangout into a full-roasted coffee date, where daydreams could turn into dinner and drinks and maybe even a late night filled with sharing secrets about our biggest dreams like how much we always wanted to be actors on the silver screen, and then we kiss like we're in a movie and one year later we're getting married while our moms are crying because they never thought they'd have grandbabies, and then we snap out of it immediately because our skin is curdling from the sight of each other faster than the oat milk is on the cappuccino that we ordered from that steaming hot barista that we secretly hope was on this date instead" question that has cost me so much money, that I should have bought a café to get return profits on all my failed relationships.

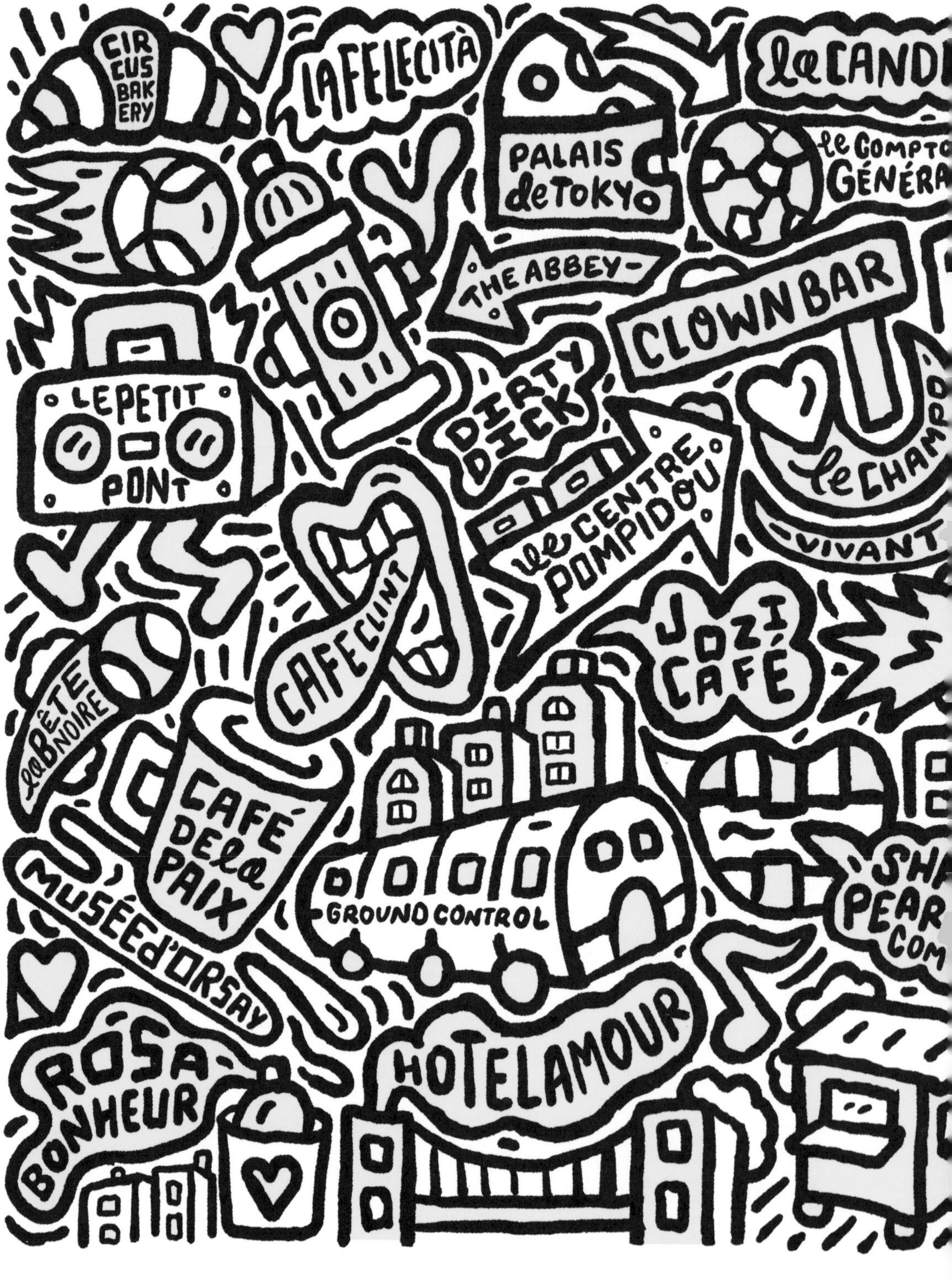

CIRCUS BAKERY
LA FELECITÀ
PALAIS de TOKYO
THE ABBEY
CLOWN BAR
LE PETIT PONT
DIRTY DICK
le CENTRE POMPIDOU
VIVANT
CAFE CLINT
JOZI CAFÉ
la BÊTE NOIRE
CAFE DE la PAIX
GROUND CONTROL
MUSÉE d'ORSAY
ROSA BONHEUR
HOTEL AMOUR

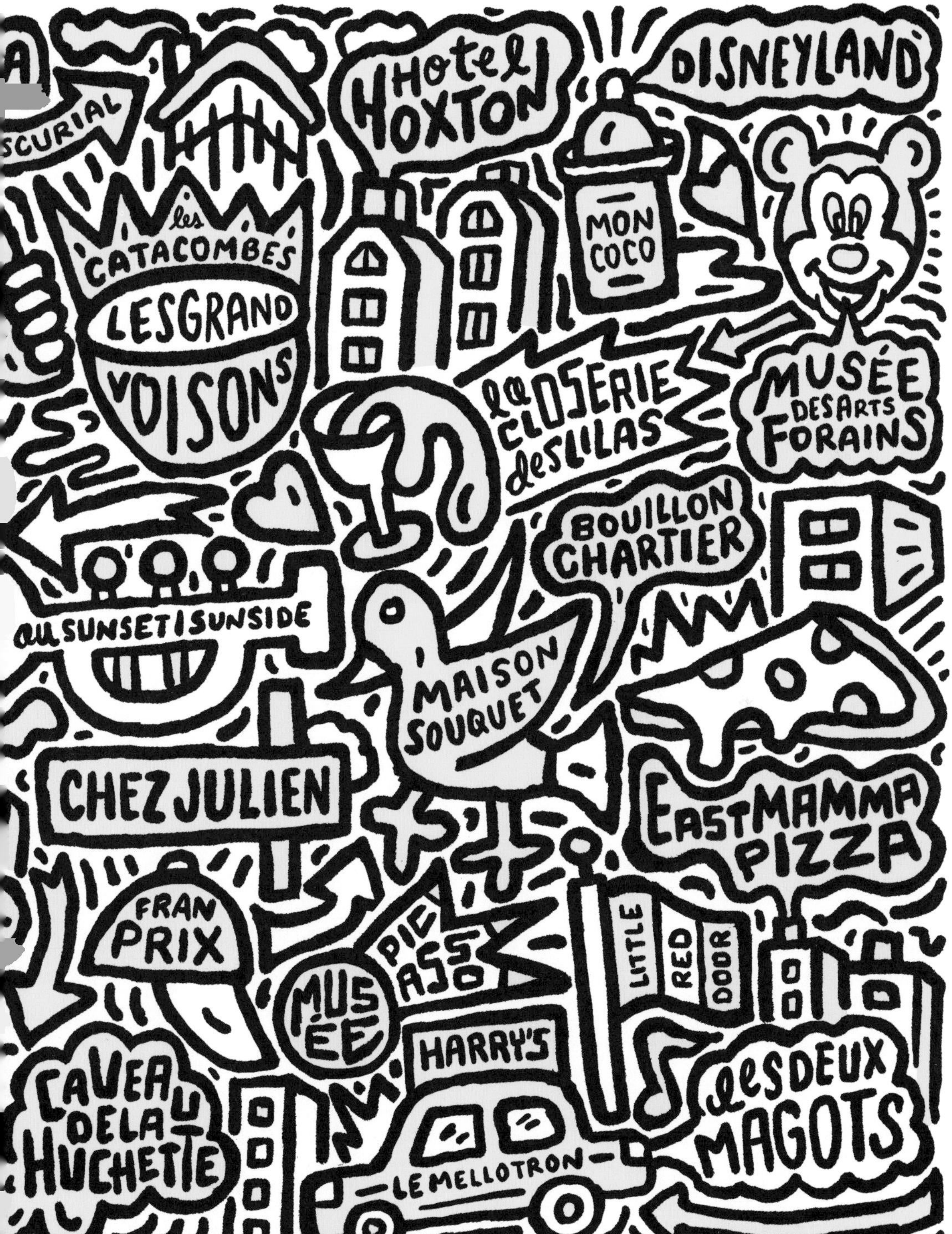

A
SCURIAL
Hotel HOXTON
DISNEYLAND
les CATACOMBES
MON COCO
LESGRAND VOISONS
la CLOSERIE des LILAS
MUSÉE DES ARTS FORAINS
BOUILLON CHARTIER
au SUNSET SUNSIDE
MAISON SOUQUET
CHEZ JULIEN
EastMAMMA PIZZA
FRAN PRIX
PICASSO
MUSÉE
LITTLE RED DOOR
HARRY'S
CAVEAU DE LA HUCHETTE
LE MELLOTRON
les DEUX MAGOTS

CHAPTER 3
INFATUATION

Prince sang "I wanna be your lover . . . I wanna turn you on . . . I wanna be the only one you come for . . . I wanna be your mother" in his 1979 hit single "I Wanna Be Your Lover." Well, I wanna be more than her lover, I wanna love her like if love could love. I wanna love more than just her heart. I wanna love all her scary parts. Like her farts, and her snorts, and everything that makes her hurt. I wanna pay the balance on whatever breaks her heart. I wanna stay up way too late having heart-to-hearts. I wanna double down on this part because I don't believe love can ever tear us apart. I don't wanna hide behind my flaws. I don't wanna be another man too scared to tear down my bullshit facade. I don't wanna go to fancy dinner parties and talk about New York real estate, organic farming, directions to work, or buying summer houses on the Annecy lake. I wanna make bad decisions and great mistakes. I wanna share some unhealthy shit like frites and shakes. I don't wanna be civilized, well-mannered, a petting animal, or a pawn for them to dismantle. I don't wanna be anyone's good example. I wanna see everything she is and everything she wants to be. I wanna show her all my faults and fears so I can be seen. I wanna cause a scene like Tom Cruise jumping on couches inside the TV screen. I don't wanna run away or play it too cool like I did all those other times. I wanna run down the Parisian streets with her hand inside of mine. I don't wanna be wise and in love at the same time, I wanna bend these rules and act like a fool in love until the end of time. I don't wanna bend over backwards for anyone who won't leave their baggage at the door, I wanna carry all her organic cotton reusable grocery bags to her front door. I don't wanna go hiking in fields or swim up streams. I wanna feel what it feels like to walk inside her dreams. I wanna be her dreamboat floating down the Seine and the Seven Seas. I wanna give her all five oceans and the four seasons. I wanna tell her that she makes me feel the opposite of blue. I wanna scream out "I love you."

CORNY
ASS
LOVE IS
REAL
AS FUCK

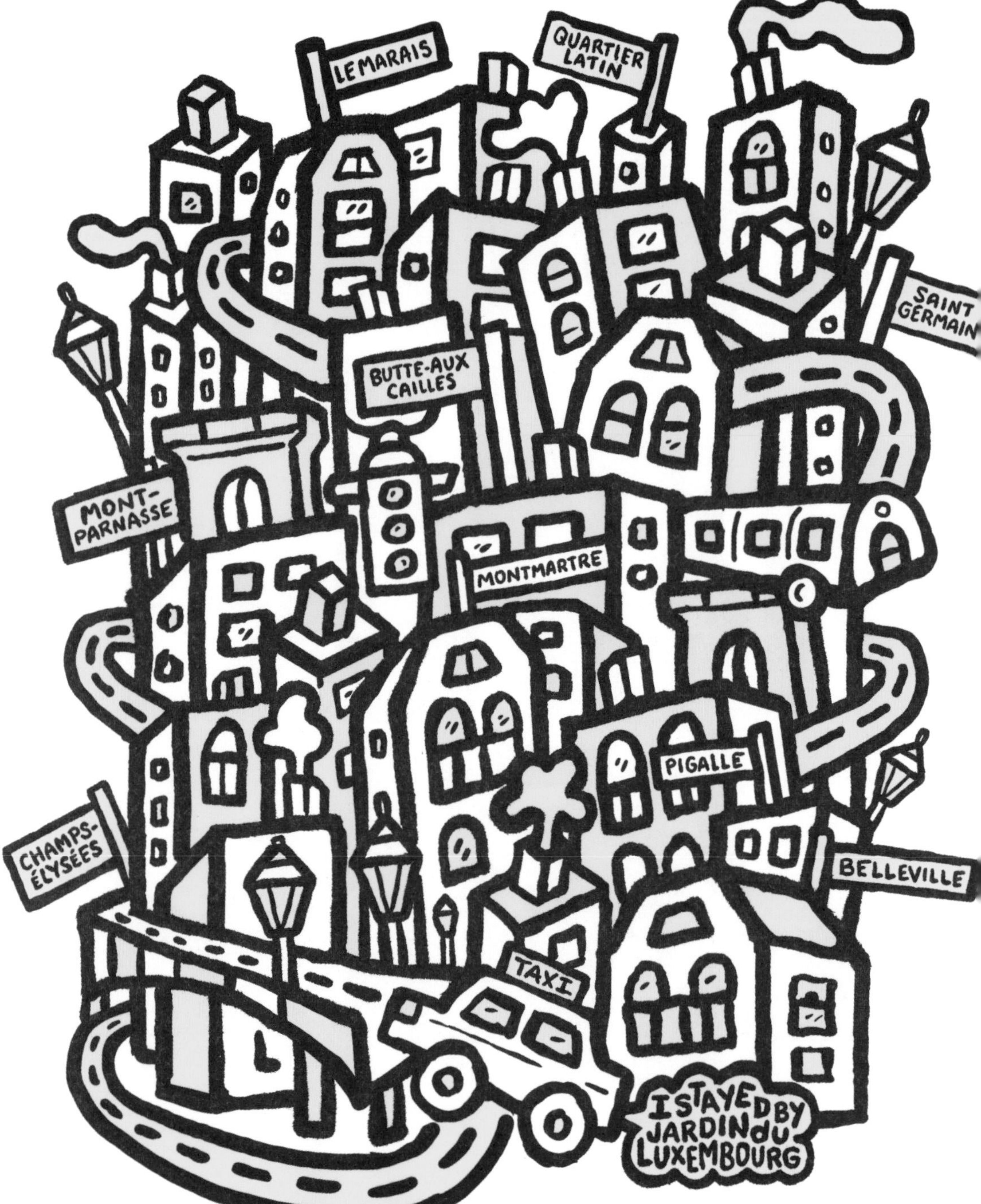
LE MARAIS
QUARTIER LATIN
SAINT GERMAIN
BUTTE-AUX CAILLES
MONT-PARNASSE
MONTMARTRE
PIGALLE
CHAMPS-ÉLYSÉES
BELLEVILLE
TAXI
I STAYED BY JARDIN du LUXEMBOURG

JULY 25

MOST MORNINGS AFTER MY RUN, I STOP AT MY BOULANGERIE TO BUY A FRESH CROISSANT. I TRY TO SPEAK TO HIM IN A LITTLE FRENCH, HE SHAKES MY HAND, AND IN HIS CUTE ENGLISH ACCENT, HE ASKS ME HOW MY FAMILY IS. HE TELLS ME THAT HIS DREAM IS TO VISIT NYC. HE ASKS ME QUESTIONS ABOUT IT: ARE THERE REALLY LOTS OF PEOPLE? WHAT'S THE WEATHER LIKE? WHAT'S THE BREAD LIKE? IS IT REALLY EXPENSIVE? IS IT DIRTY? SOMETIMES HE ASKS ME ABOUT BEYONCÉ AS IF I KNOW HER (IN HIS DEFENSE, I KINDA ACT LIKE I DO). AFTER LIVING IN NYC FOR 15 YEARS AND TRAVELING ALL OVER THE WORLD FOR WORK, I'M LUCKY THAT I RARELY FEEL DISPLACED. HOWEVER, IT'S PEOPLE LIKE MY BOULANGER WHO MAKE ME FEEL LIKE I'M AT HOME HERE. I'M MEANT TO BE EXACTLY WHERE I'M AT, THAT I'M MEANT TO BE LIVING THE LIFE I HAVE RIGHT NOW.

ON AND ON

You know when your friend asks you to send
some pictures of the new person you're so
excited about, so you carefully go through their
Instagram photos and screenshot the ones that
are fun but serious, classy but sexy, adventurous
but modest, and then you throw in a couple
comments about how they're super smart but
not uptight, that they fight for everything that
is right, how they have impeccable style but also
volunteer at a soup kitchen because they have
a deep perspective on what matters in the world,
and maybe you mention that they speak a couple
languages and have traveled all over the world,
but that they're also lowbrow and enjoy a basketball game and an IPA in a dirty bar, and you
reiterate how much you really raise the bar, that

you and your new partner are gonna go so far, that this isn't like those other people you dated thus far, those other pictures, those other texts where you went on and on about how amazing they are, that you've learned so much from your therapist who put you on to all your issues with your past relationships, and all the dirt, the busts, the disappointments, the mistakes, the outtakes, the retakes, the heartaches, and you feel so confident that your friend now knows that you're dating the most well-rounded and amazing person who's probably ever walked the earth, maybe the only living person left in New York, and you top it all off with a bunch of exclamation points just in case they didn't get the point, and then your friend finally writes back and says something like, "They're okay, but hey Tim, as long as you're happy!"?

JULY 28

THINGS THAT ARE DIFFERENT IN MY LIFE NOW:

I BOUGHT 6 BANANAS, FRESH SQUEEZED ORANGE JUICE, BLUEBERRIES, TWO CROISSANTS, AND A BAGUETTE FOR €12. I THINK THIS WOULD COST ME ABOUT $500 IN NYC.

I SEE MY FRENCH TUTOR, SANDRA, 2 TO 3 TIMES A WEEK (SHE'S THE BEST.)

I LISTEN TO FRENCH INTERNATIONAL RADIO EVERY MORNING. (SANDRA TELLS ME I NEED TO.)

I COOK SOMETHING MOST DAYS. (IS A SALAD, A BAGUETTE, AND OLIVE OIL CONSIDERED COOKING?)

I USE A BIRD SCOOTER TO GO EVERYWHERE. (IT'S LITERALLY CHANGED MY LIFE.)

DID I **MENTION** BAGUETTES? I EAT
A BAGUETTE A DAY. BREAD LAWS!!

TMI, BUT WHEN **WIPE** MYSELF, NOTHING COMES
OUT ON THE TOILET PAPER. (NOTHING'S PROCESSED!)

I READ 3 BOOKS IN A MONTH. I HAVEN'T
READ THAT MANY IN THE LAST YEAR.

I HAVEN'T WATCHED YOUTUBE **OR** NETFLIX
OR CABLE TV ONE TIME!

I CAN'T **FIND** ANY GOOD PEANUT BUTTER!
EVERYONE HERE EATS THIS LOTUS SPECULOOS
SPREAD WHICH IS BASCALLY A **COOKIE** BUTTER
GRAHAM CRACKER SPREAD. AND I HATEEEE IT LOL.

IN JULY, IT DOESN'T **GET** DARK UNTIL 10:30 PM.
THANK GOODNESS FOR HIGH LATITUDE.

SOMETHING- I'M-NOT

I grew up in an all-Black neighborhood for my first 13 years. Then, suddenly, we moved towns and I was going to school with white kids who called me "Goodman" like I was in *The Wonder Years*. On the first day of my new school, I wore the dopest two-piece Jordan outfit with the shoes to match, too. I remember Peter asked me in second-quarter science class what my last name was. I looked at him and said, "Something I'm not." I seriously said that, trying to be dope. That entire year kids made fun of me for being something I was not: them. They beat me up. They made fun of how I walked, how I talked, how my mom picked me up every AM in a beat-up Grand Am. I would cry in my bedroom and tell myself that I'll prove them wrong one day. I told myself that if

I could somehow just be "me," that I'll be "some-one" one day. Even though I really didn't see a way out, I would have voted "no way" to ever making my way out with the pictures I make or the words I write. Eventually I made some friends. I played a little sports. I quit sports. I started smoking weed every day to avoid dealing with my mom's recent divorce. I barely graduated. I went to jail three times. I tried every drug to escape time. I couldn't get into a college. I painted homes in Cleveland for four years. And then I became infatuated: with making it, with making my way out, with making work that would make my mom proud, with making something that would make my entire soul shout. And yes, I wanted to make those kids who had no respect for my name to remember my name now. The memories of my father who was never around, my first stepdad who would throw me around, my second stepdad who suddenly started coming around, I worked around the clock to prove to everyone that I was going to move on. So, I moved to NYC to go to design school at SVA, graduated at 27, and 10 years later I finally realized the "success" I had came, in large part, because I was only reacting to my broken heart. And it's important to myself that I'm honest about what used to make my clock tick because in the future I don't want to witness my time slip away too quick. Now, as I experience and have access to joy more and more, I'm still trying to process it all. I'm still trying to let go.

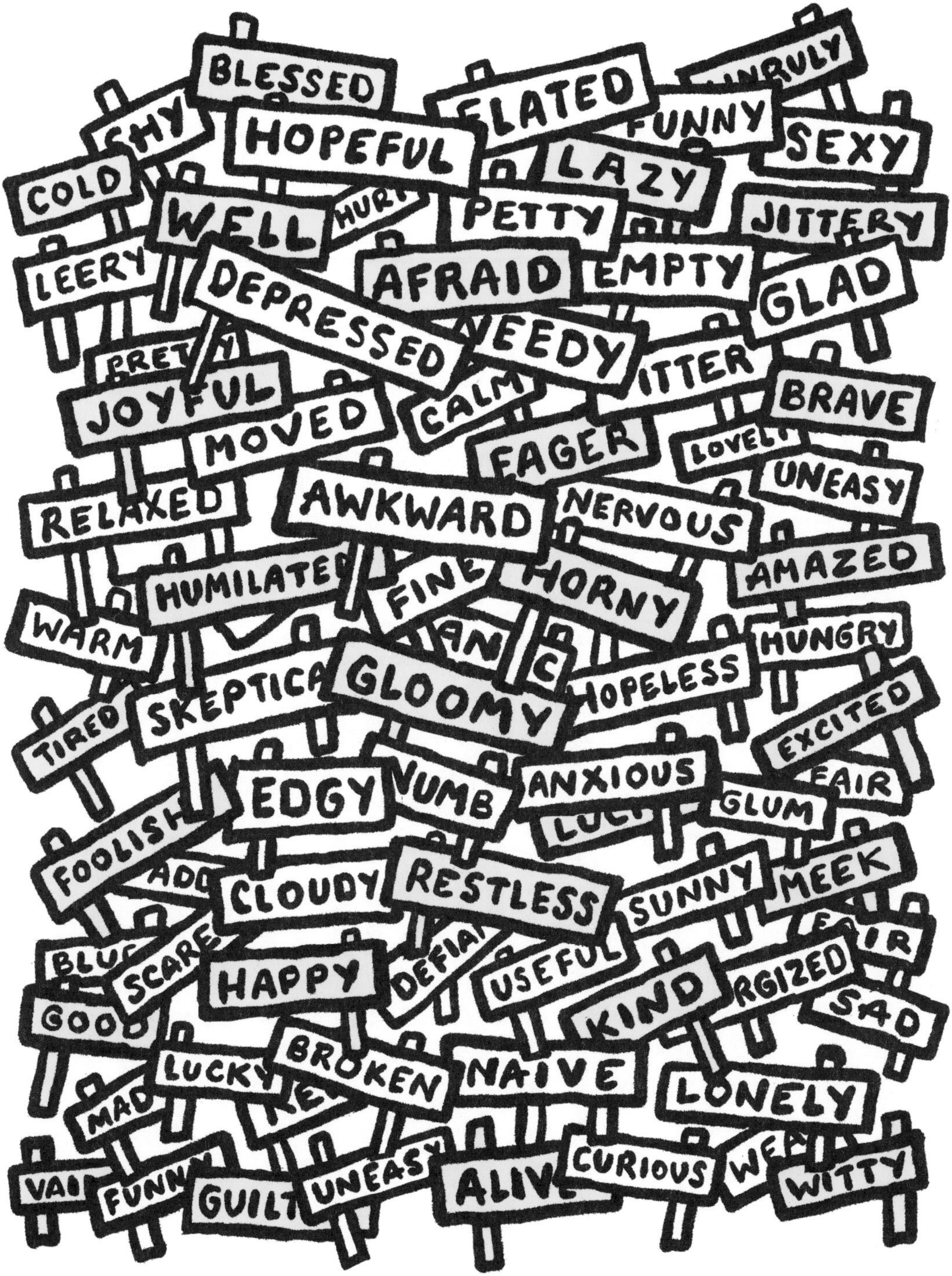
BLESSED
ELATED
UNRULY
SHY
HOPEFUL
FUNNY
SEXY
COLD
LAZY
WELL
PETTY
JITTERY
LEERY
DEPRESSED
AFRAID
EMPTY
GLAD
NEEDY
JOYFUL
CALM
BRAVE
MOVED
EAGER
UNEASY
RELAXED
AWKWARD
NERVOUS
HUMILATE
FINE
HORNY
AMAZED
WARM
HUNGRY
GLOOMY
HOPELESS
TIRED
SKEPTICA
EXCITED
EDGY
NUMB
ANXIOUS
FAIR
GLUM
FOOLISH
CLOUDY
RESTLESS
SUNNY
MEEK
SCARE
HAPPY
USEFUL
RGIZED
KIND
SAD
LUCKY
BROKEN
NAIVE
LONELY
MAD
CURIOUS
WITTY
FUNN
GUILT
UNEASY
ALIV

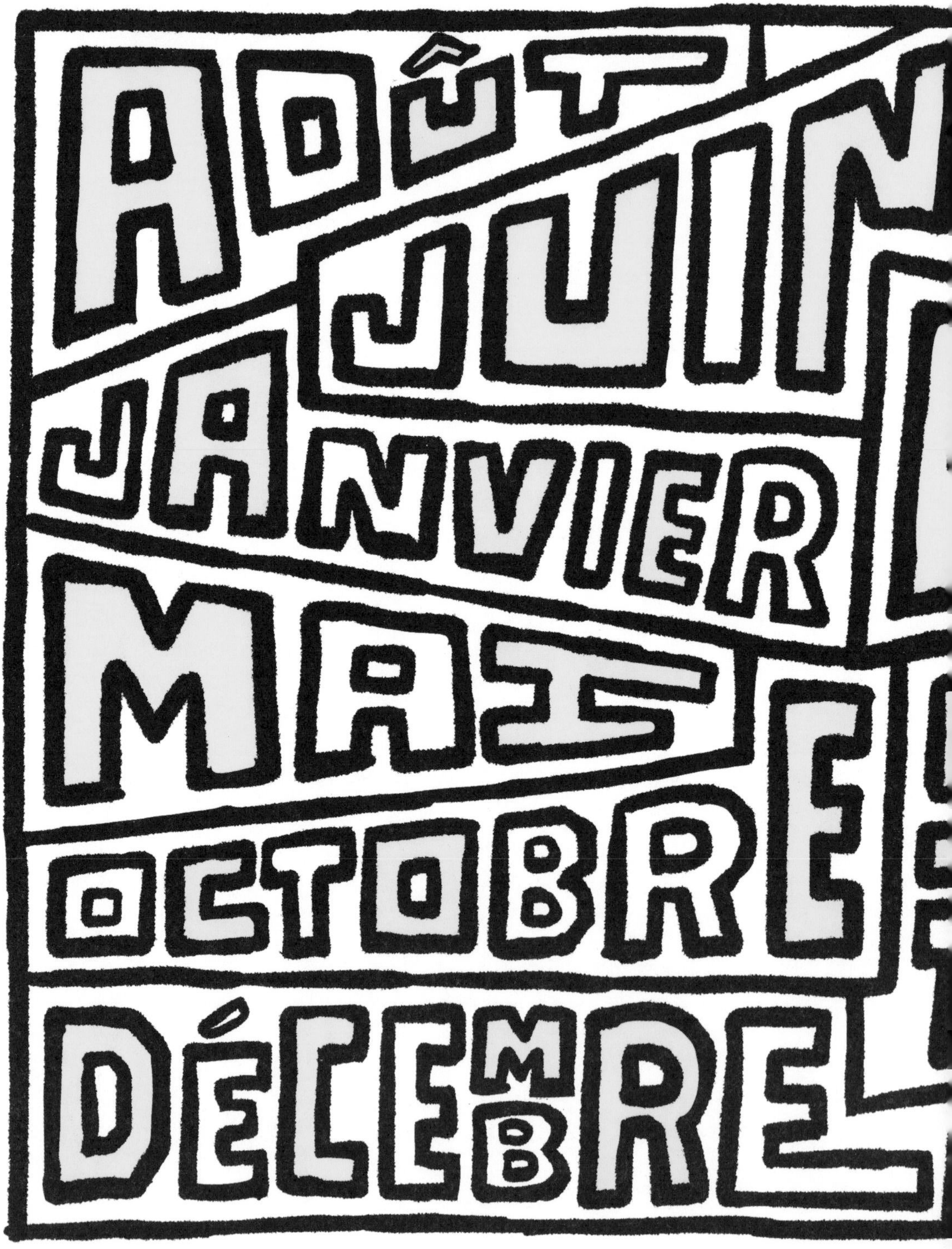
AOÛT
JUIN
JANVIER
MAI
OCTOBRE
DÉCEMBRE

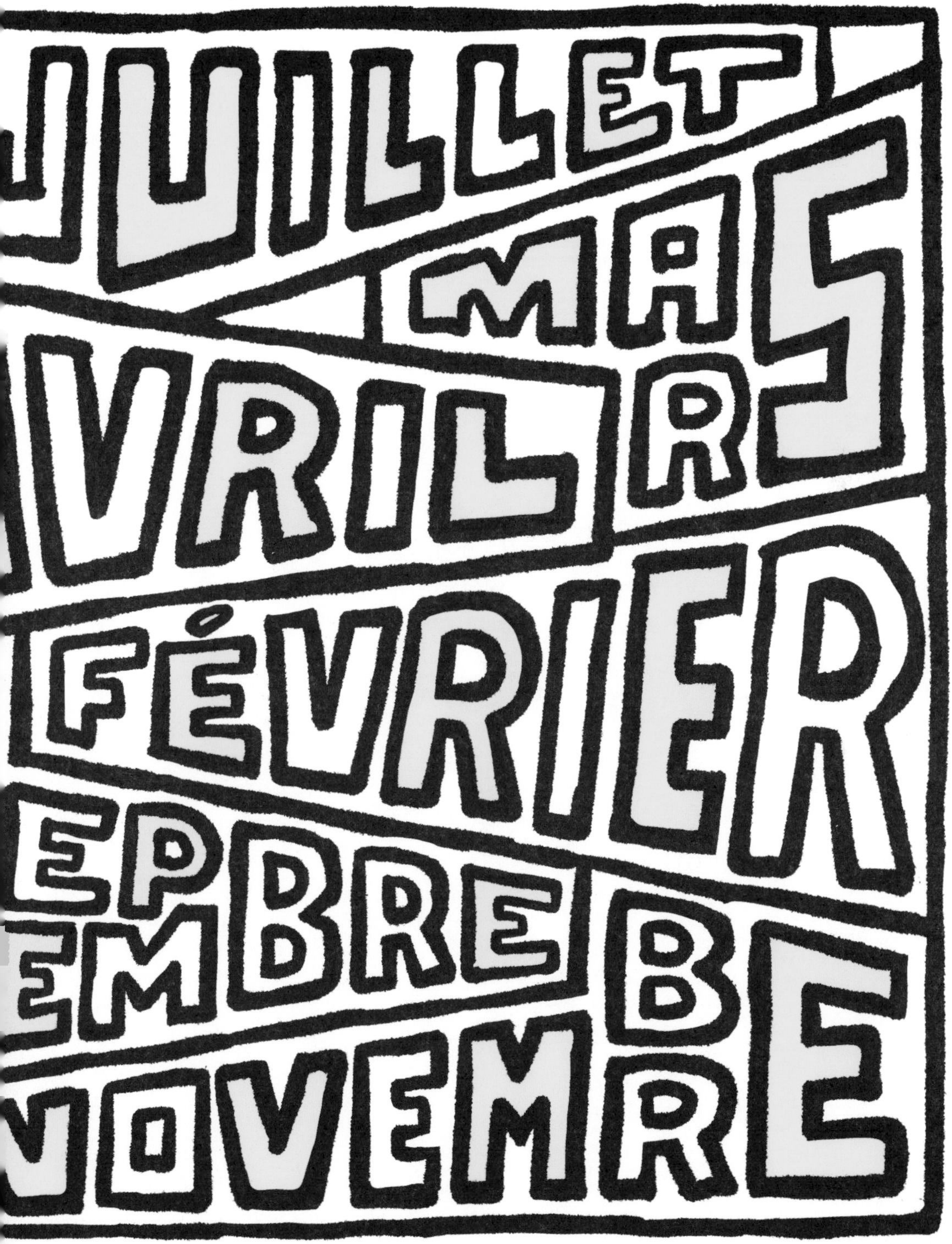

JUILLET
MA S
VRIL R
FÉVRIER
EPBRE
EMBRE B
VOVEMR E

CHAPTER 4

FALLING

e'd only been on a couple dates, but I immediately changed my return ticket back to the United States to a later date. Call it crazy or call it great, but we were having a week like *Call Me by Your Name*, and she was calling me "baby" every day. I called that Delta operator and told her exactly what was in my heart. She said, "Baby, don't you think you could be taking this too far? You've only known this girl for a week, don't play all your cards!" I said, listen, Pam, sometimes you gotta roll the dice to win it despite the high stakes, sometimes you gotta look past your past despite how long your last heartbreak lasted. I look back at my past and can't believe I never put it all on the table, I can't believe I spent so many meals talking across tables when we weren't saying anything real. And unlike that other Timothée, this Timothy is real, and Aimée was the real deal. She got me so head over heels that I needed to stay, way past the summer, because I was talking like a little baby despite what I say. Pam said, "You mean, talking like a baby, like goo

goo and ga ga?" I said, ma'am, I'm talking like the French say "ooh la la." She took a pause and laughed a little, then she said, "Sir, hold for one moment so I can fiddle with the flights a little." For one long little minute I waited on that line, telling myself if this relationship doesn't work out, I'll be fine. That going after love has no fines, that my intuition never lies, that it's no big deal to prolong my trip for a short little while. Then I thought about it awhile longer and I told myself that I should probably slow my roll. That I really need to get back home, that I don't have some sorta love syndrome, that I should read a great book about patience, that this was all a crazy idea anyway, that I've only known this woman for like 13 days! Then I decided that I'm gonna hang up the call and call it a day. The operator Pam got back on and said, "Sorry, babe, but this flight is actually gonna cost you double from what you initially paid." I said, I guess that's the price for love, so please, ma'am, book it today!

LOVE IS UNDEFEATED

FIRSTS

FIRST TIME you get BUTTERFLIES MEETING THEM EVEN if IT'S THE 5TH TIME SEEING THEM

FIRST TIME you CUT YOUR TOE NAILS SO THEY DON'T think YOU'RE THE KIND PERSON WHO DOESN'T CUT THEIR TOENAILS REGULARY

FIRST TIME you FIND OUT THEY DONT LIKE SOMETHING AMAZING like PIZZA and YOU CAN'T UNDERSTAND it BUT you REALLY THINK IT'S THE CUTEST THING in THE WORLD

FIRST TIME YOU ASK a QUESTION THAT YOU DO NOT WANNA KNOW the ANSWER TO

FIRST TIME you THINK you BETTER NOT MESS UP

FIRST TIME you MESS UP

FIRST TIME YOU FEEL it SLIP AWAY AND YOU KNOW YOU CAN TRY HARDER BUT you DON'T

FIRST TIME you PUT A SWEATER on THAT YOU HAVEN'T WORN IN a LONG TIME & IT SMELLS LIKE THEM

FIRST TIME you HEAR a CHEESY BREAKUP SONG IN CVS AND IT MAKES you SAD

FIRST TIME you HOPE YOU RUN INTO THEM BECAUSE YOU'RE LOOKING GOOD THAT DAY

FIRST TIME you HOPE you DON'T RUN INTO THEM BECAUSE YOU'RE LOOKING ROUGH THAT DAY

FIRST TIME you HOPE YOU DON'T RUN INTO THEM BECAUSE YOU'RE FEELING GOOD THAT DAY AND YOU DON'T WANNA RUIN IT EVEN THOUGH YOU DO WANNA RUN INTO THEM OR YOU WOULDN'T BE THINKING ABOUT IT ANYWAYS

FIRST TIME you THINK ABOUT THOSE TIMES THEY WOULD TEXT YOU ON THEIR WAY HOME LATE at NIGHT AND HOW THEY'RE PROBABLY DOING THAT with SOMEONE ELSE

FIRST TIME you REALIZE YOU'VE STOPPED THINKING of THEM

FIRST TIME BECOMES just ANOTHER FIRST TIME

AUGUST 4

THE DAY BEFORE EVERY LESSON, MY FRENCH TUTOR, SANDRA, TEXTS ME, "BONJOUR TIMOTHÉ! J'ESPÈRE QUE TU VAS BIEN. A DEMAIN!" THIS TEXT ALWAYS FILLS ME WITH A MIX OF EXCITEMENT AND ANXIETY BECAUSE I KNOW IT MEANS I'M GONNA HAVE TO FACE THAT DREADED FEELING OF REALLY STRUGGLING AT SOMETHING. HOWEVER, IT'S SO POWERFUL TO FEEL LIKE I DON'T KNOW SOMETHING, TO FEEL LIKE I WON'T EVER "GET IT." LIVING IN A FOREIGN CITY AND LEARNING A NEW LANGUAGE CAN STIR UP DIFFICULT FEELINGS OF HUMILIATION, BUT WHAT EVENTUALLY ARISES, FOR MYSELF, IS A STRONG CURIOSITY AND A CHILDLIKE WONDER. SIMILAR TO A FIRST DATE, OR TELLING SOMEONE YOU LOVE THEM FOR THE FIRST TIME, OR WHEN I WENT TO DESIGN SCHOOL, OR MOVED TO NYC, OR STARTED WORKING FOR MYSELF. THE AUDACITY TO LET YOURSELF FEEL SCARED AGAIN. HOW BEAUTIFUL. OUR HEART HAS AN INTELLIGENCE THAT OUR MIND CAN'T BEGIN TO COMPREHEND, AND SOMETIMES YOU MUST BLINDLY FOLLOW ITS LEAD.

EMERGENCY EX

Talking to the Delta operator made me think about my first international flight after my ex and I broke up the previous year. Rather than simply clicking "check in" on my Delta app, like I usually do when I travel domestically, I was required to verify all my information at the kiosk at JFK airport. This process asked me to confirm whether my emergency contact was still the same. My ex was my emergency contact. I honestly didn't even remember that she was, but now I have this greasy-ass kiosk reminding me about my failed relationship, which was not only rude, but also really quite embarrassing. I mean, if I had died in a plane crash in the several months since breaking up, she would have been the first person the authorities contacted. Not my mom or my best

friend or my grandma or my second-best friend.
No, it would have been her: someone who didn't
want to be my emergency contact anymore, someone who was someone else's emergency contact.
I'm already a person who gets very sentimental
while traveling, someone who cries to *The Intern*
on a two-hour-long flight to Chicago, so I really
could have done without this reminder. Anyway,
I'm happy I didn't die and I made it to London.

FIRST THING YOU NOTICED ABOUT your PARTNER

"THE WAY EVERYTHING SLOWED DOWN WHEN SHE LOOKED at ME and THE WAY HER SMILE RADIATED THROUGOUT MY ENTIRE BODY."

 "I NOTICED HER LAUGH. SHE was FULL of ENERGY, HAVING FUN WITH HER BEST FRIEND. THEY WERE JUST ANNOYING FOLKS AROUND THEM, INCLUDING ME. NOW 8 YEARS LATER I CAN'T EXIST WITHOUT HER LAUGH."

"THE WAY HE LOOKED at MY WHOLE FACE. I HAD NEVER BEEN LOOKED at LIKE THIS."

"HIS GORGEOUS AFRO and UGG SHORTS. I HATED THOSE SHORTS."

"I NOTICED HOW SHE NOTICED me. TO ACTUALLY BE SEEN. IT WAS SO SCARY and MADE ME FEEL SO ALIVE."

"THEY WERE'NT AFRAID to MAKE A FOOL OF THEM SELF in ORDER TO MAKE KIDS LAUGH."

"I'D BEEN FEELING SUICIDAL ATELY. SHE CRACKED A OKE and DISARMED ME WITH THE MOST EASING AUGH & SMILE i've SEEN."

"HIS KINDNESS. HE SPOKE TO ME and SOME FRIENDS at A TRAIN STATION in JAPAN. I HAD JUST GOTTEN OUT OF A BAD RELATIONSHIP and I WAS QUESTIONING A LOT. AND WHEN I MET MY PARTNER, he REMINDED ME THERE are STILL PEOPLE WHO are GENUINE."

CHAPTER 5
TRUST

imée never saw a Scorsese movie or had a peanut butter and jelly sandwich, and we never talked much about world politics. She rolled her pants up, not really for fashion, but because she bought them too long from the thrift store. Her hair was down to her ass, but she always put it up when we talked about important shit like why her mom and dad split up or her love for early 90s hip-hop. She seemed to care so much about everything that she didn't care about anything, and she told me she'd rather stay broken than end up with a broken heart. Her legs connected to her pelvis, but I swear they were really connected to some other universe where I didn't have to feel rejection or disappointment, and I didn't have to reject or disappoint. I asked about her last relationship and she said, "Memories change with time just like the impressions of the lovers we leave behind," as she took a sip of her red wine. I think the lovers we feel the most connected to are the ones that touch our emotions and mind, and I was attracted to the sadness in

her eyes because sadness is a part of life, and that shit made me feel so fucking alive. It was then that I knew everything would be fine; all those times I'd trip because I had nobody to come home to after a long work trip, nobody to ask me what we should eat for dinner. As we finished our dinner, I told her I was trying to find truth in Paris, she said whether I do or I don't, to just not follow the same patterns (and that I should follow the astrology app, The Pattern).
I thought about all those drunken summer nights I weathered when I was younger. I thought about how my grandparents are getting so much older. I put a jacket over Aimée's shoulder because the night was becoming colder. I felt how much I was falling for her, so I told her. I had to let go of all my little fantasies because this was bigger.

IN THE FUTURE EVERYONE WILL KISS THEIR CRUSH

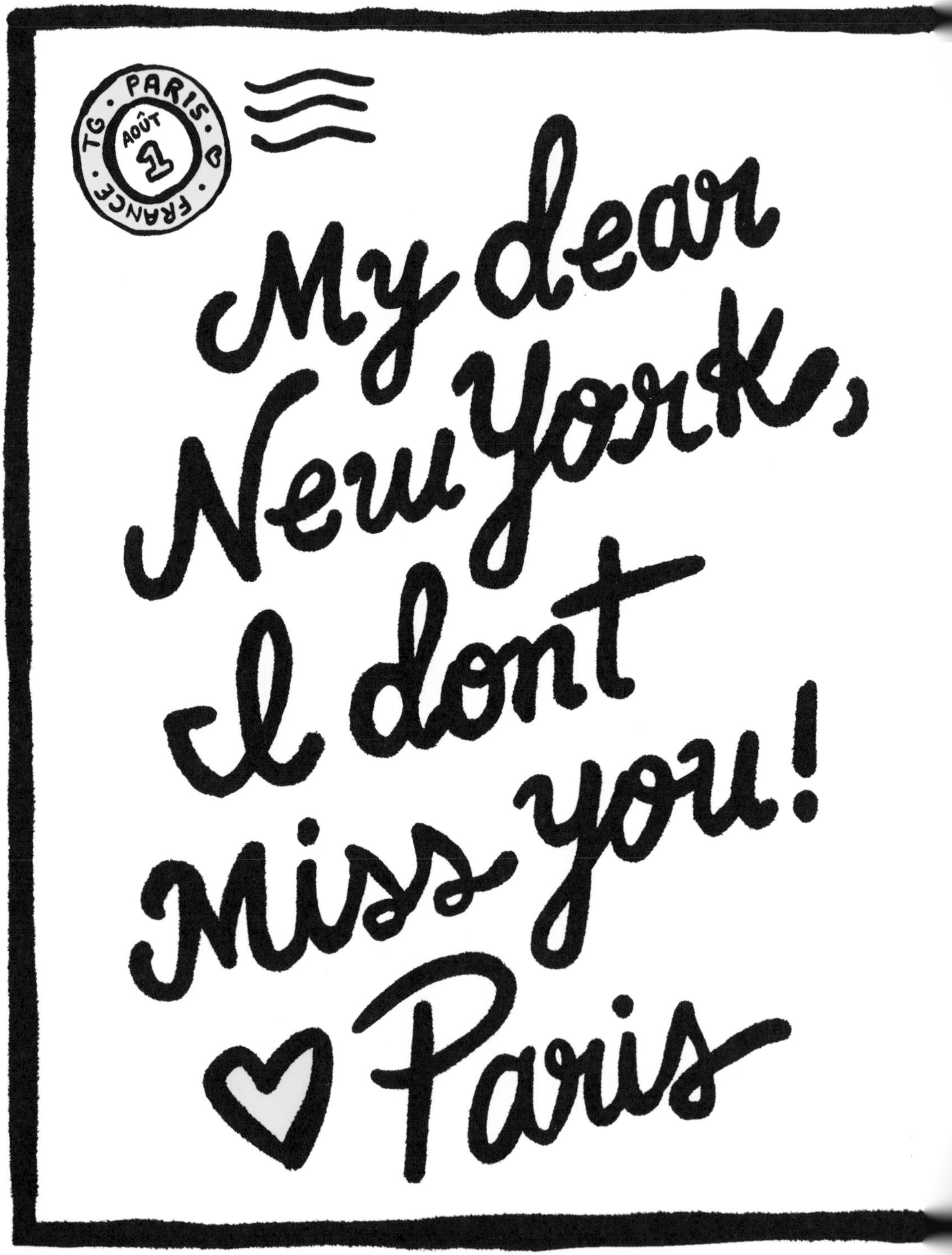
PARIS · TG · FRANCE
AOÛT 1
My dear New York, I dont miss you!
♥ Paris

AUGUST 22

THE BIGGEST DIFFERENCE BETWEEN PARIS AND NEW YORK? FOLKS DON'T CASUALLY DATE HERE THE WAY THEY DO IN NEW YORK. IN PARIS, IF YOU GO ON THREE GREAT DATES WITH SOMEONE AND IT'S CLEAR YOU BOTH LIKE EACH OTHER, THEN YOU'RE PRETTY MUCH EXCLUSIVE. NOW, THAT DOESN'T MEAN IT HAS TO BE SUPER SERIOUS RIGHT AWAY. IT JUST MEANS THAT YOU'RE BOTH COMMITTED TO SEEING IF THIS CAN BE SUPER SERIOUS. THERE ARE NO GAMES OR TALKS. YOU'RE JUST... TOGETHER. IT'S SO REFRESHING AND UNCOMPLICATED. THE OTHER DIFFERENCES? THERE IS NO AC HERE, WHICH I'M GOOD WITH, BUT IT WAS 104 DEGREES THE OTHER DAY AND I ALMOST DIED LOL. OH, ALSO, SEEMINGLY EVERYBODY SMOKES CIGARETTES. AND I CAN'T GET GOOD (I.E., BOUGIE) PEANUT BUTTER ANYWHERE. FINALLY, WHY DO THE FRENCH NOT HAVE A NEW WORD FOR THE NUMBER 90!? THEY LITERALLY SAY "FOUR-TWENTY-TEN." THIS IS SO UNNECESSARY, I THINK I'M GOING TO WRITE TO THE CONSULATE RIGHT NOW.

ELEVEN WORDS

It's that one word "Hello" that turns into two words
"You're cute" that I always hope becomes three
words "I love you" but all too often the story ends
with four words "Go fuck yourself, Tim" because
maybe these five words "Do you have a condom?"
should stop happening before six important words
like "Maybe we should take it slow" and then I
could stop asking myself seven words like "When
will I ever get it together?" or yelling eight words
at myself like "You stupid-ass idiot, you lost a great
girl!" and simply understand these nine words first:
"Treat them the way you want to be treated" and
also learn ten words like "Don't be hard on yourself, it will all work out" and then maybe one day
I'll be ready for these eleven words: "Do you take
this woman to be your lawfully wedded wife?"

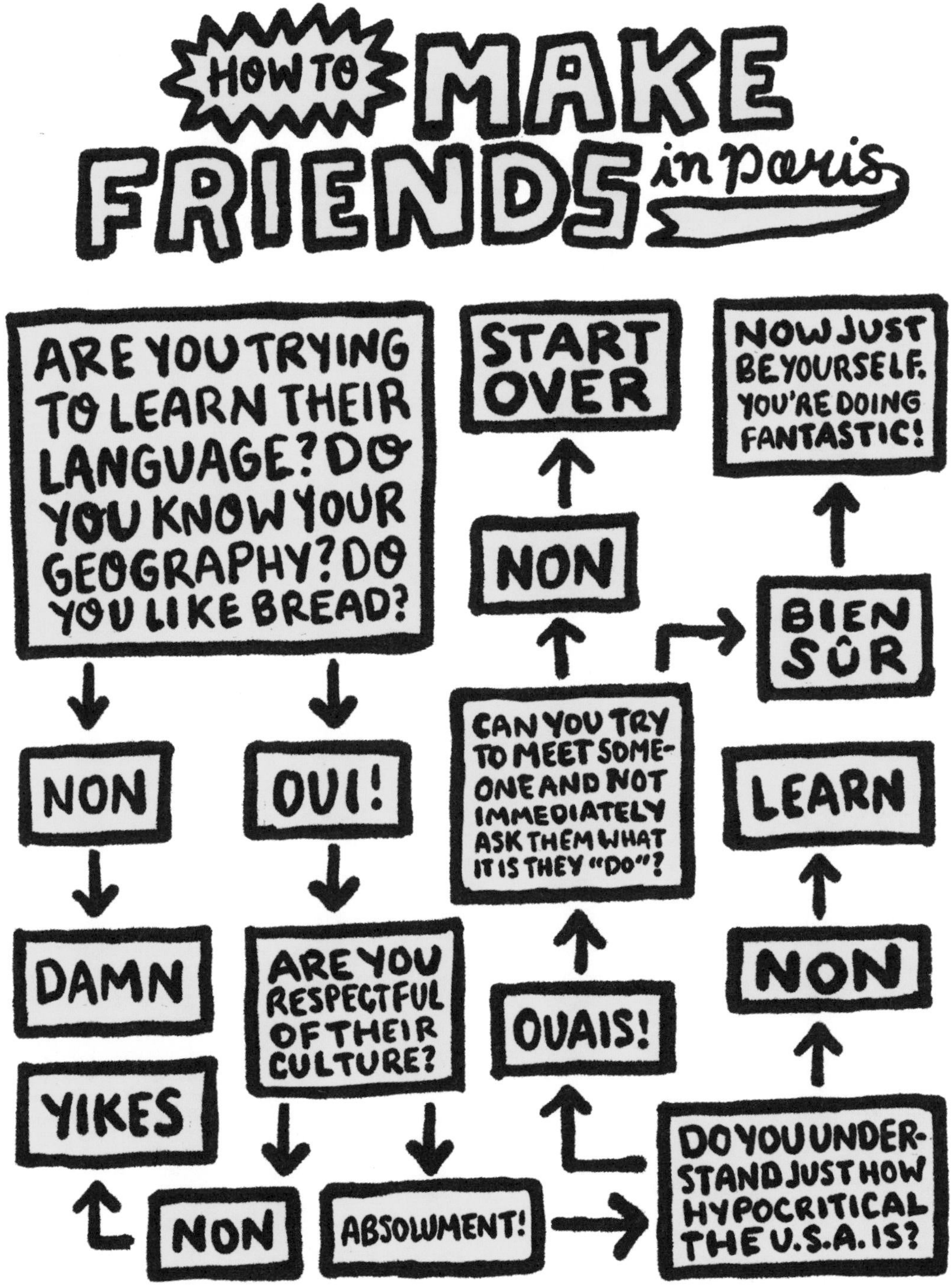
HOW TO MAKE FRIENDS in paris
ARE YOU TRYING TO LEARN THEIR LANGUAGE? DO YOU KNOW YOUR GEOGRAPHY? DO YOU LIKE BREAD?
NON
DAMN
YIKES
OUI!
ARE YOU RESPECTFUL OF THEIR CULTURE?
NON
ABSOLUMENT!
DO YOU UNDERSTAND JUST HOW HYPOCRITICAL THE U.S.A. IS?
NON
LEARN
OUAIS!
CAN YOU TRY TO MEET SOMEONE AND NOT IMMEDIATELY ASK THEM WHAT IT IS THEY "DO"?
NON
START OVER
BIEN SÛR
NOW JUST BE YOURSELF. YOU'RE DOING FANTASTIC!

It's that ONE word " HELL

WORDS "YOU'RE CUTE" THAT I Q

THREE WORDS "I LOVE

the STORY ENDS WITH FO

YOURSELF, TIM 99

WORDS "DO YOU HAVE A CONDOM

BEFORE SIX IMPORTAN

WE SHOULD TAKE it SLO

ASKING myself SEVEN h

OR YELLING EIGHT WORDS

IDIOT, YOU LOST A GREAT GIRL!"

NINE WORDS FIRST "TREAT

learn TEN WORDS LIKE "DI

IT WILL ALL WORK OUT"

BE READY FOR THESE ELEVEN

HAT TURNS INTO TWO
ys HOPE BECOMES
... BUT all TOO OFTEN
R words "GO FUCK
ause MAYBE THESE FIVE
HOULD STOP HAPPENING
WORDS like "MAYBE
AND THEN I COULD STOP
DS LIKE WHEN WILL I EVER GET IT TOGETHER?
MYSELF LIKE "YOU STUPID-ASS
UD simply UNDERSTAND THESE
m the WAY YOU WANT to BE TREATED" AND also
T BE HARD ON YOURSELF,
THEN Maybe ONE DAY I'LL
ds "DO YOU TAKE this WOMAN to BE your LAWFULLY WEDDED WIFE?

CHAPTER 6

MERGING

She was my first real love in years, and as I cooked breakfast for her in my underwear, I realized I hadn't cooked breakfast for anyone in years. Not even for myself, not even for my ex, not even when I was so depressed last year that I blew off every girl I met out of fear. We talked about our families, we laughed about astrology, we danced all over my Airbnb, the sun came up and the night came in and we woke up at noon and did it again. And as the light broke through a broken shade, we laid in bed naked talking about how broken I've been. I told her all about the depression I had. She told me about the messiness in her head. I could smell the scent of her saliva all over my skin. I could feel my heart turn inside out from within. I could hear the ghosts of my past relationships say "Farewell, my friend." We must have made love a hundred times over again: in the bed, in the shower, on that huge wooden table as we knocked over the flowers. I met her friends, we danced all night, we ate, we drank, we hung on the back of motorbikes, we hung all over each other like all of Paris was painted in black and white. She grabbed my hand as we walked into a karaoke place, my world became Technicolor when I kissed her face. I asked her what she thought we were living for, if we could reach our potential, if we could grab everything that's in front of us. And here she is in front of me asking, "What is it about us broken ones? Like dried up petals, or puddles of rain, there's something so inane but yet so possible." And I didn't know it was possible to feel okay with being so perfectly broken as we laughed, sang, and selected her favorite Britney Spears songs from a cracked screen. I felt my fractured heart scream out for the love I need. Then she whispered something cute in French that she knew I wouldn't understand. I whispered to myself, "I never want this feeling to ever end."

HEART ACHE IS JUST A REWRITE OF YOUR HEART'S STORY

THE HEART WANTS what it WANTS

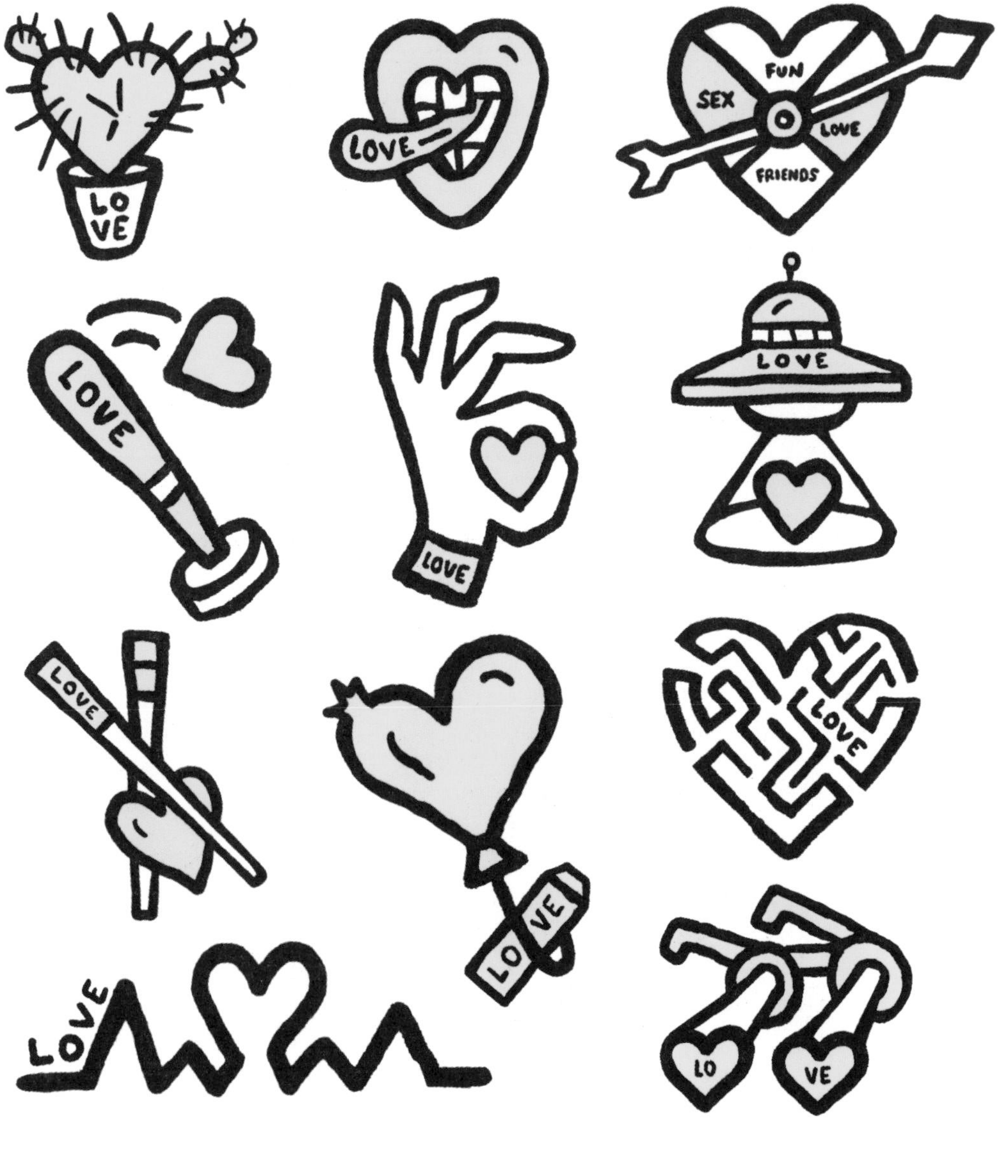

LO VE
LOVE
FUN
SEX
LOVE
FRIENDS
LOVE
LOVE
LOVE
LOVE
LOVE
LOVE
LO VE
LOVE
LO
VE

SEPTEMBER 6

I **JUST** LEARNED THAT THE WORDS "MAGIC WAND" LITERALLY TRANSLATES TO "BAGUETTE MAGIQUE" IN FRENCH. I LOVE SANDRA FOR TEACHING ME THIS. THERE IS A CAT THAT IS ALWAYS HANGING **OUT** IN THE COURTYARD OF MY BUILDING, AND IT MAKES ME FEEL LIKE I'M LIVING IN A MOVIE. SHE SPEAKS FLUENT FRENCH, SPANISH, AND ENGLISH. I **THINK** LE CHAT USES A BAGUETTE MAGIQUE. YESTERDAY, I ACCIDENTALLY RAN INTO A HOMELESS GUY'S CUP OF CHANGE AND I FELT HORRIBLE. HE MUST HAVE BEEN IN HIS EARLY 20S. **HE** ASKED ME TO BUY HIM SOME FOOD AT MCDONALD'S, SO I **BOUGHT** HIM A BIG MAC, FRENCH FRIES, AND A CHOCOLATE MILKSHAKE. HE WAS ROMANIAN AND DIDN'T SPEAK MUCH FRENCH OR ENGLISH AT ALL. I ASKED OUR SERVER FOR THE "FRACTURE" INSTEAD OF "L'ADDITION" AND I FELT DUMB, EVEN THOUGH **SHE** WAS VERY NICE ABOUT IT. ANYWAY, IT'S CHILLY AT NIGHT HERE SO I GO TO BED WITH THE WINDOW CRACKED OPEN AND IT SMELLS LIKE HALLOWEEN. THEN IT GETS WARM DURING THE DAY AGAIN. I **FEEL** LIKE A LITTLE KID.

SPINNIN'

After a late night out with Aimée I stumbled
across Le Jardin du Luxembourg, so I lay on the
grass and I accidentally stumbled on this video
of my ex spinning around on the grass in front of
these lights one night after a play we went to
one summer we went upstate, and you can hear
me saying "spin baby spin" as she spun around
so happily, but sometimes it's not so easy to look
back at videos where she looked good and I was
happy, because even though now I'm spinning
the world with one finger I'd be a liar if I said the
presence of her didn't still linger, in my world, in
my head, in the way I carry this new relationship ahead, and sometimes all my messy feelings
blend together like West Coast seasons that
never end, because every new love has to begin

after the last one ends, and I guess I needed in-
between time to work on all my loose ends, so
like an old friend, I wanna meet again, I wanna
make amends, I wanna hit send on that thoughtful
email and give that story a storybook bookend,
because without her I woulda never truly grown,
I would have never been able to admit that I
wanted so much more, even tho I know another
half isn't supposed to make me whole, but this
time around I'm not gonna run on cruise control,
so I watched that video and now I know that I'm
grateful I got to spin with her before she had to go.

CORNERS

I WALKED *by* THIS CORNER WE WALKED *on* DURING OUR FIRST DATE.

FRUIT

FIGUE | POMME | BANANE | TOMATE

frais

I WONDERED *what your* NEW CORNER IS WITH YOUR NEW GUY & HOW *many* MORE CORNERS YOU'LL HAVE BEFORE *you* FIND THE —— RIGHT GUY. ——

I WONDERED *if* THESE CORNERS WILL HAUNT ME ALL *the* TIME *or* IF I COULD SOMEHOW TRY TO FORGET EVERY THING LIKE 'ETERNAL SUNSHINE OF *the* SPOTLESS MIND' *or* MAYBE I'M JUST LOSING MY MIND.

KATE WINSLET

I WONDERED WHY I AVOID the STREETS THAT GET ME to WHERE I WANNA GO on TIME & I WONDERED HOW MANY TIMES I'LL TURN CORNERS in ORDER to AVOID MY LIES.

I WONDERED WHY I WASN'T your RIGHT GUY & THEN I WONDERED why I CUT CORNERS ON OUR RELATIONSHIP WHEN I just COULDA BEEN a BETTER GUY.

I WONDERED if I'LL BE THE RIGHT GUY EVER TO ANYONE at ANYTIME or IF I'LL KEEP WALKING BY CORNERS and LOOKING —BACK AT TIME.—

CHAPTER 7
L'AMOUR

I waited outside her apartment for an hour thinking about that cute little birthmark on the left side of her cheek, while I simultaneously Googled all the ways I could tell her I love her in French. Do I say "I love you" or do I say "Je t'aime" or do I say them both back-to-back like the Splash Brothers before they got Kevin Durant? I texted my French tutor and asked her if there was something I was missing. Is there another way to tell her how much I miss her when I'm not with her? She said, "Listen, just treat this exactly like your art. There's no translation for what's inside your heart. Besides, French women love when a man knows exactly what he wants." So, when Aimée arrived, I told her how she makes me feel like I have no sense of time, no past, no future, not a thing that ever reminds me of the life I left behind. I told her that I want to make this work even if I have to go back to NYC for work. I told her that even tho we haven't known each other for so long, I can't worry about my fears of her saying "So long." I told her that I know time ain't short and I need to stop longing for the past all the time. I told her that in the past I couldn't get past the weight of my past, that I was always looking for any excuse to grab my passport and fly past anything that could potentially break my heart into glass. I told her that looking at her is like looking directly at the sun, and the way we talk all night makes me think about our future daughter and son. I told her I had something important to say, that I never felt that way, that the feeling of falling for her that way in a city like Paris could never fade away. And before I could utter those three little words, she shut the door, she looked so cute, she held me tight and said, "Shut up, please don't say anymore." Then she whispered, "Je t'aime, I love you."

I'M TOO YOUNG TO NOT SET MY LIFE ON FIRE, I'M TOO OLD TO NOT SPEND MY TIME WITH SOMEBODY I REALLY ADMIRE

My BREAK-UP TIMELINE

ME WITH MY VAGUE UNDER-STANDING OF THE HUMAN CONDITION

CRYING WHILE WATCHING the 'BEFORE' TRILOGY

CRYING WHILE READING 'ALL ABOUT LOVE' BY bell hooks

CRYING WHILE EATING a BOX of WHEAT THINS FOR DINNER

RE-ACTIVATING MY DATING APP PROFILE and SEEING THE SAME PEOPLE

MAKING the BEST BREAK-UP PLAYLIST YOU'VE EVER HEARD

4PM 6PM 8PM

ADMITTING THAT I'M ILL-EQUIPPED AT HANDLING THE EMOTIONAL CAPACITY I NEED TO BECOME a SELF-REALIZED MAN

THIS IS MY MIND AND IT'S BEAUTIFUL

ASK FOR HELP. GO TO THERAPY. CRY AGAIN!

MAKING ART ABOUT ALL MY EXPERIENCES

SEPTEMBER 27

LONELINESS CAN BE A FRIEND. I'VE BEEN THINKING A **LOT** ABOUT ANTHONY BOURDAIN RECENTLY, AND HOW MY EX AND I ONCE SAW HIM IN THE ELEVATOR AT THE CHATEAU MARMONT. I WAS IN LA ON THE DAY HE DIED OF SUICIDE, GETTING **READY** TO GO TO A MOSCHINO FASHION SHOW WITH A WOMAN I WAS DATING WHO LIVED THERE. SO, I WAS TAKEN ABACK LATER THAT NIGHT WHEN MY DATE WANTED TO GO TO THE **CHATEAU** TO MEET SOME OF HER FRIENDS. WHAT WERE THE CHANCES I WOULD END UP AT THE SAME PLACE I ONCE SAW ANTHONY ON THE SAME DAY THAT HE KILLED HIMSELF? IT FELT SURREAL. I HAD BEEN STRUGGLING WITH DEPRESSION FOR OVER TWO MONTHS AT THAT POINT, AND I HAD **CASUALLY** FANTASIZED ABOUT SUICIDE. AS WE DROVE BACK TO HER **HOUSE** THAT NIGHT, I TOOK THIS AS A SIGN TO GET MORE PROACTIVE WITH MY MENTAL HEALTH. BUT THAT DOESN'T MEAN I DON'T STILL FEEL A WAVE OF LONE-LINESS WASH OVER ME BEING HERE IN PARIS BY MYSELF. IT'S A DOUBLE-EDGED SWORD; **THAT** LONELINESS CAN FEEL YUCKY, BUT A LOT OF TIMES IT'S WHEN I'M THE MOST CREATIVE, IT'S WHEN I FEEL THE MOST ALIVE.

MATT DAMON

That LA lady was the kinda lady you'd see in the
movies because I actually saw her in the movies,
so when she asked me to fly to LA for one night
to see her IRL, it was like something you would
only see in the movies. So, what did I do? I rented
a 1968 Mercedes-Benz because that's what I
would do if this was a fucking movie. Flying down
the Pacific Coast Highway, the ocean on her
right side, I couldn't believe this incredible
woman was next to me as the hair blew in her
eyes. As we kissed in a dusty bar on a fire-orange
Malibu night, I remember she smiled a smile
that I'll never not remember. I remember she
made me feel like I could finally join a club that
would have me as a member. It's that corny-ass
love that is real as fuck, so I put my chips on the

table for the chance for something real, even if it was luck. Even if in reality I was flying away from the memories of losing something real, the reality of that past rejection made me feel like I wasn't worthy of the real deal. Sometimes the only way to heal a broken spirit is to jump on that plane, even if it's Spirit Airlines with a connection in the Kansas Plains. I was on that Matt Damon "I gotta go see about a girl" shit, flying to LA like I was the shit. And for one night, I felt like I was living in a movie when this amazing lady I saw in the movies was with me, Timmy G. I'm too young to not set my life on fire, I'm too old to not spend life with someone I admire, so I'm gonna jump on more planes until my miles or my heart expires.

WHENYOUR
ONEANDTHEY
LIKEYOUYO
EVERYTHING
KNOWTHEY'
INGABOUTA
YOU'LLMOVE
THINGTOSOM
OVERTHINKEV

LLYLIKESOME
ON'TREALLY
OVERTHINK
BECAUSEYOU
ENOTTHINK
YTHINGSO
NTOBESOME
ONEELSEAND
RYTHINGAGAIN

CHAPTER 8
COMMITMENT

I came to Paris to free myself from what I knew so I could see myself more clearly. I had no idea that would include falling in love with a woman who would take my heart's greatest hits and hit Library>History>Clear. So let me be even clearer. The last year was my worst personal year, so this year I was determined to confront all my fears: to learn the French language, to live my life like I was the lead character in my favorite foreign language movie, to simply make decisions that favored my well-being. I finally did things for me. Not for my career, not for some facade that I could never keep up out of fear. And then I met Aimée, with her smile, her heart, the picnics we had at Tuileries park, the way she surprised me with a trip to Disneyland after I mentioned it when I was drunk, and all we shared in those months. Suddenly everyone's asking questions like: Am I moving to Paris? Is she moving to New York? How do you have a plan to make it work? Can a long-distance relationship across the Atlantic Ocean in two different countries with a six-hour time difference really work? Aren't you too old for this, it seems like a lot of work? All I knew is that I'd only ever been young, but I was finally thinking about the bigger picture. I was thinking about wedding pictures. I was thinking about a second house on the Hudson River. I was thinking about giving our kids trendy names like Hudson and River. For the first time in years, I felt like I was meant to be living the life I had, and no matter what happened between the two of us from there, I knew I was committed to her. Unlike other times, I would never let our relation-ship end because I was too scared to put myself out there. In French, instead of saying "I miss you," they say "Tu me manques," which literally translates to "You are missing from me." And by that time tomorrow, I'd be gone, and after all the searching, I'd be back in the city I started from. Only that time she'd be missing from me . . . but not for very long.

THE MORE
I FIND
MYSELF
THE MORE
I LOSE
MYSELF

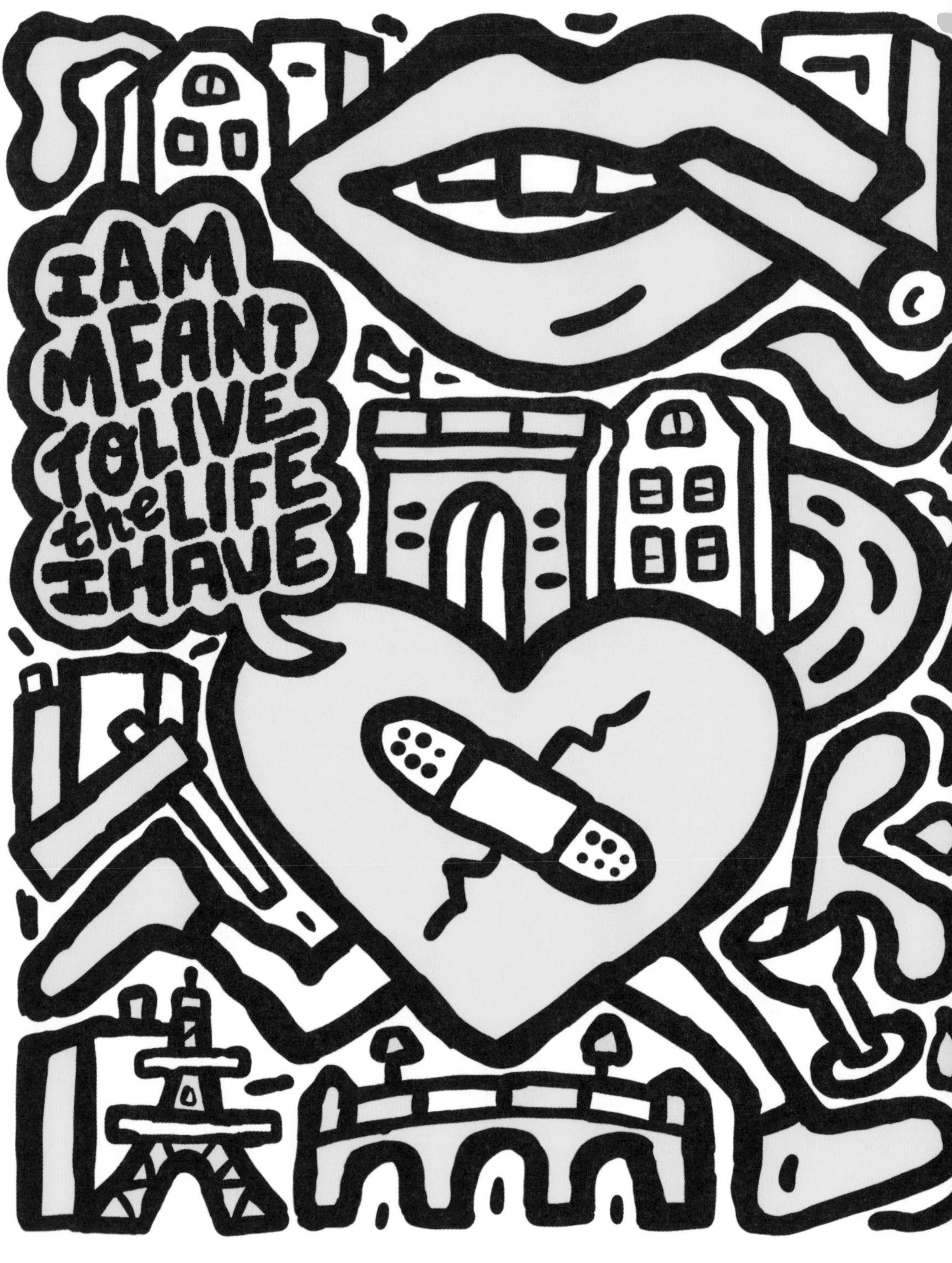
I AM MEANT TO LIVE the LIFE I HAVE

OCTOBER 30

TODAY I'M LEAVING PARIS AFTER SPENDING FOUR MONTHS TRULY LIVING FOR THE FIRST TIME IN MY ADULT LIFE. AIMÉE TAUGHT ME ABOUT THIS OLD FRENCH WORD "ROCAMBOLESQUE," WHICH DOESN'T REALLY TRANSLATE TO ENGLISH BUT DESCRIBES A WINDING AND ADVENTUROUS STORY THAT IS UNIMAGINABLE, FANTASTICAL, AND UNBELIEVABLE. THIS WAS ME LIVING THE GREATEST SUMMER OF MY LIFE, FEELING AS IF I HAD NO PAST OR FUTURE AS I WAS LEARNING FRENCH AND EATING ALL THE BAGUETTES. THIS WAS ME FINDING SOMETHING I DIDN'T EVEN KNOW I WAS LOOKING FOR. NOW MY HEART IS BURST- ING WITH SO MUCH LOVE. I BELONG LIVING THE LIFE I'M LIVING, AND I HOPE EVERYONE CAN FIND THAT FEELING MORE AND MORE. AS I GOT IN THE CAR FOR THE AIRPORT THIS MORNING, IT STARTED TO RAIN. IT WAS SO WONDERFUL LOOKING OUT AT THE WET PARISIAN STREETS WASHING AWAY ALL I EXPERIENCED FOR THIS NEXT CHAPTER. À BIENTÔT, PARIS. MERCI POUR MA VIE.

EVERY RELATIONSHIP is EITHER a TORNADO OR a HURRICANE. WHILE BOTH FOLLOW the SAME WEATHER PATTERN, HURRICANES ARE much STRONGER AND RARER BASED on WIND INTENSITY.

IN OTHER WORDS,
HURRICANES REALLY
TEAR shit UP. THAT'S
WHY EACH HURRICANE
GETS A **NAME.**

SO, IF I WAS in A RELATIONSHIP FOR SIX MONTHS WITH AIMÉE, DOES that MEAN SHE'S MY "EX"? WHY CAN'T SHE JUST BE "SOMEONE I DATED for SIX MONTHS" INSTEAD? I MEAN, DID we GARNER ENOUGH INTENSITY TOGETHER? YES, I am LEFT WITH QUITE A BIT OF INTERNAL DAMAGE and DEBRIS TO CLEAN UP NOW. IT'S REALLY NO BIG DEAL THAT I CAN'T EAT or SLEEP, OR THAT I HAVE THIS DEEP PIT in THE BOTTOM OF MY STOMACH THAT is WALLOWING FROM THE DEPTHS of ETERNAL ADELE SONGS HELL.

SO YEA, I GUESS THERE *is* A DIFFERENCE BETWEEN BEING MY "EX" AND BEING "SOMEONE I DATED ~~for~~ SIX MONTHS," BUT IS AIMÉE REALLY MY EX? I THINK SHE WAS JUST a LITTLE TORNADO THAT HAD ABSOLUTELY, POSITIVELY ZERO EFFECT on ME WHATSOEVER. SO PLEASE ENJOY THE SECOND PART OF *this* BOOK THAT I WROTE ABOUT OUR RELATIONSHIP.

PAP

ROME, ITALY

RT2
_____
NEW YEAR'S

CHAPTER 9

SHOCK

We sat together at a bar, and got to know each other a little, but little did we know we would kiss in a little while. As we walked along the Seine at 2 AM, we laughed at the drunk guys who jumped in. Neither of us knew that our summer would become consumed. Our lives. Our bond. Our fun. We became our moon and our sun. But after I went back to NYC, we both felt too far away. Her bones didn't feel it all the way. My lips didn't have the words to say. So, we tried to mask the hurt. Two people who loved each other, just not enough to make it work. After a couple months away, I woke up in an empty room in Rome on New Year's Day. She left that morning after we decided to part ways. We met there the day before because we were struggling to become something more than another failed long-distance song and dance. We had hopes that we could turn our summer romance into another chance. I guess walking around different European cities together wasn't the best plan. It took just 36 hours to throw in the towel. So, I threw the covers on the floor and covered up my face, took a deep breath, and felt that empty hole deep in my chest. I couldn't even get dressed, but I wanted to change everything, I wanted to know if she really meant something. Did I have the means to say what was meaningful? Would I give every cent I had to make sense of all that? How was I gonna pay the balance on my broken heart, and why couldn't I hear my therapist telling me it wasn't my fault? How was I gonna break this constant cycle? How could I cycle through my overwhelming thoughts thoughtfully? Could I admit how much it really hurt me? Could I face the facts, no FaceTimes and texts, just face-to-face at face value without saving face? And in the end, I threw her face wash away. I deleted her off my phone's faves. I pretended everything was okay, but I still wouldn't wash the shirt I wore the day we finally walked away. The memories wouldn't wash away. I still thought about her every day. It was just the beginning of another sad love story to roll your eyes at today.

IT'SA
PRIVILEGE
TOBE
HEART
BROKEN

PLACES TO AVOID while HEARTBROKEN

LAS VEGAS
BUT REALLY ANY CASINO OR ANY CITY THAT HAS A CASINO

-A- PANDEMIC
IT'S NOT THE VIBE. AVOID AT ALL COSTS. RESCUE A PUP

SUBWAY
BUT IT'S ALSO KINDA AMAZING

YOUR JOB
NOTHING'S WORSE THAN CRYING IN A STALL WHILE @ COWORKER TAKES @ SHIT NEXT <u>to</u> YOU

CELEBRATIONS
YOU'LL GET DRUNK, SAY SOMETHING REGRETFUL ABOUT KANYE & LOSE YOUR NEW PHONE

A CRUISE
IT'S HELL ON WATER. WHY DO THESE EXIST?

*

MAYBE THIS IS A LIST OF PLACES TO AVOID GENERALLY?

JANUARY 1

WELL, NOT ONLY AM I HEARTBROKEN, BUT I ALSO HAVE THE FLU. THERE'S NOTHING LIKE CRYING AND SNEEZING IN A BOWL OF THE BEST CACIO E PEPE I'VE EVER TASTED. WHEN IN ROME, RIGHT? UPON BREAKING UP, AIMÉE LEFT ALMOST IMMEDIATELY, BUT I WON'T LEAVE FOR ANOTHER WEEK BECAUSE I CAN'T GET A TICKET THAT ISN'T LIKE A MILLION DOLLARS. SHE LEFT EARLY THIS MORNING. WE BARELY SLEPT. TEARS WERE IN OUR EYES, BUT NEITHER OF US SAID MUCH. BOTH OF US KNEW THIS RELATIONSHIP WASN'T WORKING. LONG DISTANCE IS SO HARD! AND TO MAKE MATTERS WORSE, SHE WAS UP ALL NIGHT COUGHING AND SNEEZING. NOW I'M SICK. SICK IN MY BODY. SICK OF ANOTHER FAILED RELATIONSHIP. SICK OF MYSELF. SICK OF THIS FUCKING CITY. I FLEW NINE HOURS TO COME HERE. I SPENT ALL THIS MONEY ON THE AIRBNB AND FLIGHT, AND WE BROKE UP WITHIN 36 HOURS. I'VE BEEN WALKING AROUND THE COLOSSEUM ALL DAY REPLAYING YESTERDAY IN MY HEAD OVER AND OVER. LET ME TELL YOU, I'M NO GLADIATOR. OUR ENERGY WAS OFF THE MOMENT WE MET AT THE AIRPORT. WE DIDN'T HOLD HANDS ALL DAY. NONE OF THIS MAKES SENSE. YES, THE DRAMA OF ALL THIS FEELS LIKE A MOVIE THAT I DO NOT WANT TO STAR IN.

I'M NOT GONNA

I'm not gonna write about her. I'm not gonna write about how much I miss her. I'm not gonna write about how sometimes when I can't fall asleep, I remember how I woke her up that one morning at 5 AM so I could go out and spray-paint on those quiet Parisian streets. I'm not gonna write about how cute she looked when she would leave me videos of her riding her bike during the day, or how we rode scooters together over the Petit Pont one day after we had ice cream. I'm not gonna write about how she had one of the all-time greatest smiles, how when she smiled, she smiled with real sincerity, how that shit made me feel very close to her emotionally. I'm not gonna write about her accent, her Byredo scent, or how she always encouraged me to speak to the waiters in French. I'm not gonna write about how I think she's already seeing another guy, how hard I'm taking that emotionally, how much I hate being the "last guy." I'm not gonna write about how much this wasn't working for me at the end, how busy I got with work again, how taking Paris out of the equation made me realize we're just two strangers walking around Rome trying to pretend. I'm not gonna write about how months or years with someone can feel like a glance, how I've been having a hard time since, how years of therapy doesn't always make it make sense. I'm not gonna write about how thankful I am for our time, how it made me realize I could actually do better in time, how much better I'll be with the right person next time. I'm not gonna write about her.

25 NON-CHEESY

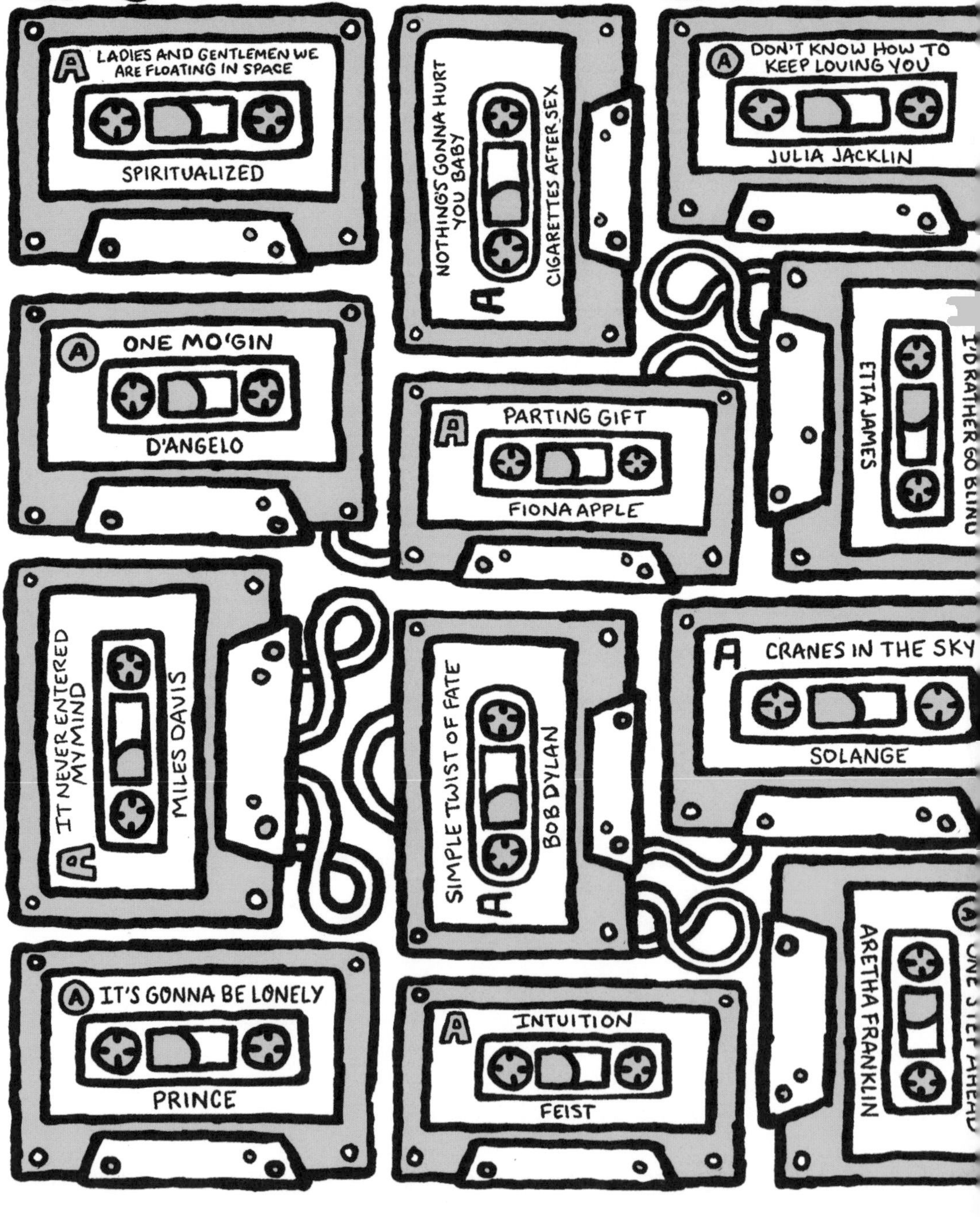
A
LADIES AND GENTLEMEN WE ARE FLOATING IN SPACE
SPIRITUALIZED
A
NOTHING'S GONNA HURT YOU BABY
CIGARETTES AFTER SEX
A
DON'T KNOW HOW TO KEEP LOVING YOU
JULIA JACKLIN
A
ONE MO'GIN
D'ANGELO
A
PARTING GIFT
FIONA APPLE
I'D RATHER GO BLIN
ETTA JAMES
A
IT NEVER ENTERED MY MIND
MILES DAVIS
A
SIMPLE TWIST OF FATE
BOB DYLAN
A
CRANES IN THE SKY
SOLANGE
A
IT'S GONNA BE LONELY
PRINCE
A
INTUITION
FEIST
A
ONE STEP AHEAD
ARETHA FRANKLIN

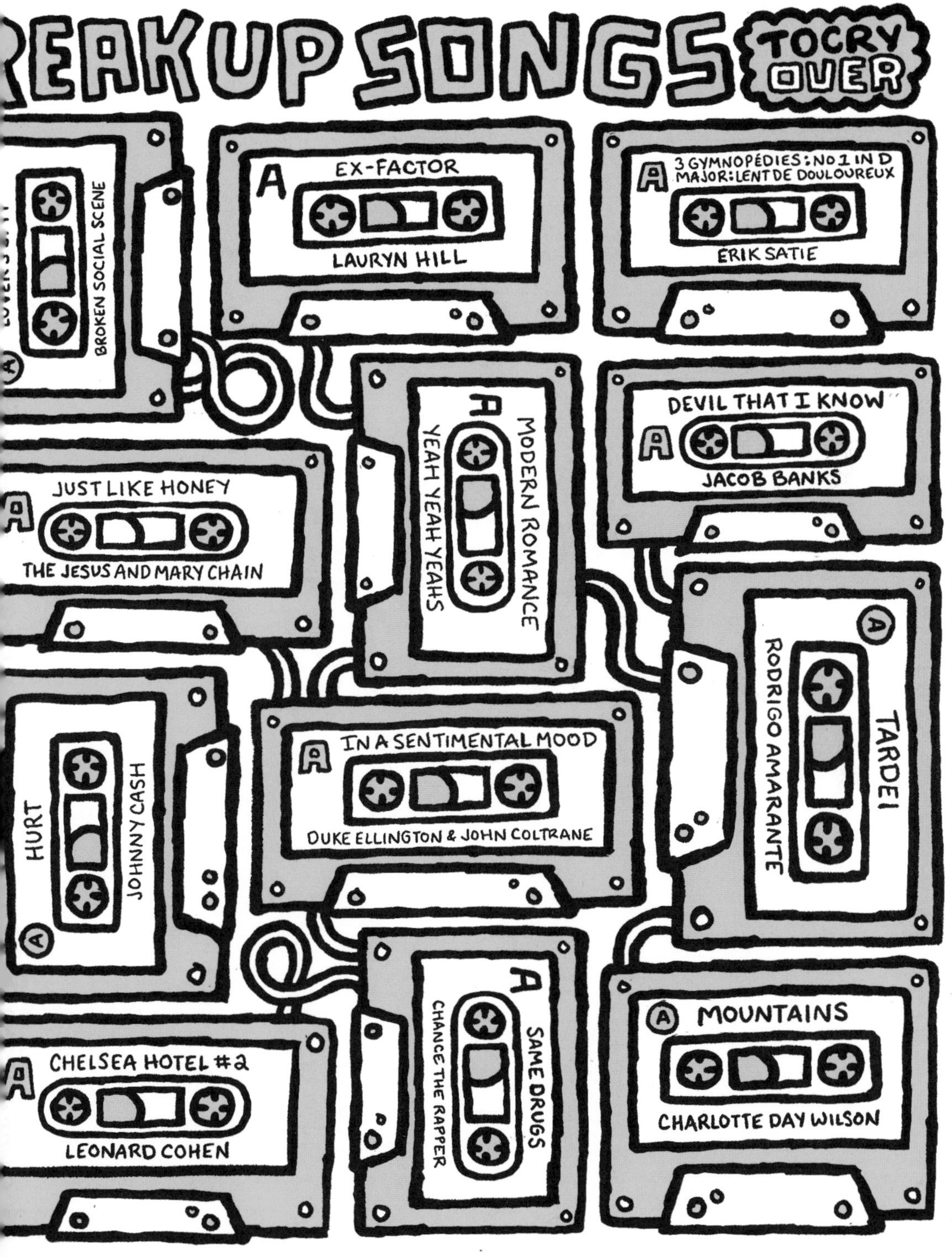
REAKUP SONGS
TO CRY OVER
BROKEN SOCIAL SCENE
A
EX-FACTOR
LAURYN HILL
A
3 GYMNOPÉDIES: NO 1 IN D MAJOR: LENT DE DOULOUREUX
ERIK SATIE
A
MODERN ROMANCE
YEAH YEAH YEAHS
A
DEVIL THAT I KNOW
JACOB BANKS
A
JUST LIKE HONEY
THE JESUS AND MARY CHAIN
A
TARDEI
RODRIGO AMARANTE
A
IN A SENTIMENTAL MOOD
DUKE ELLINGTON & JOHN COLTRANE
A
HURT
JOHNNY CASH
A
SAME DRUGS
CHANCE THE RAPPER
A
MOUNTAINS
CHARLOTTE DAY WILSON
A
CHELSEA HOTEL #2
LEONARD COHEN

CHAPTER 10

DENIAL

"Remove friend forever?" That's what it asked me when I tried to delete Aimée as my friend from the Co–Star astrology app. "Forever." I just stared at that word on my screen for minutes as I thought about why she and I didn't last forever. I thought about how we looked at our compatibility charts on our first date, right after the Vietnamese we ate right by Place de la République. I thought about how it made me happy when we had a moon sign in common, thinking it was a sign of the things to come. I thought about how we lay under the stars in Bordeaux and laughed about how our moms loved that Phil Collins song "Against All Odds." I thought about how the app told us that against all odds, with five smileys and no frowns, that our relationship would totally work if only we were committed to making it work. I thought about the notifications that would pop up on our phones like that one time we were eating popcorn during *Once Upon a Time in Hollywood*, and boy did I feel like the last living boy in Hollywood and Paris combined, because no one was going to tell me that she wasn't going to be mine. And I thought about how I felt when it all fell apart, knowing we both could have done so much more. "Remove friend forever?" is such a definitive question that leaves me feeling startled because I never imagined an astrology app would be the final confirmation of us walking away forever. I mean, what if we got back together? What if the stars aligned again, we made amends, and we became great friends? But if I proceeded with this app, I knew there was no turning back. There's no horoscope hack that can change this fact. Yes, my emotional Cancer ass only always forgets to think before I act. I make villains and narratives in my head so I can get ahead. My momma taught me that. Never mind that, I hit the button, looked out at the sky, and tried to forget about the regrets I felt inside.

YESTER
DAY, TOD
AY & TOM
ORROW
PLAY TO
GETHER

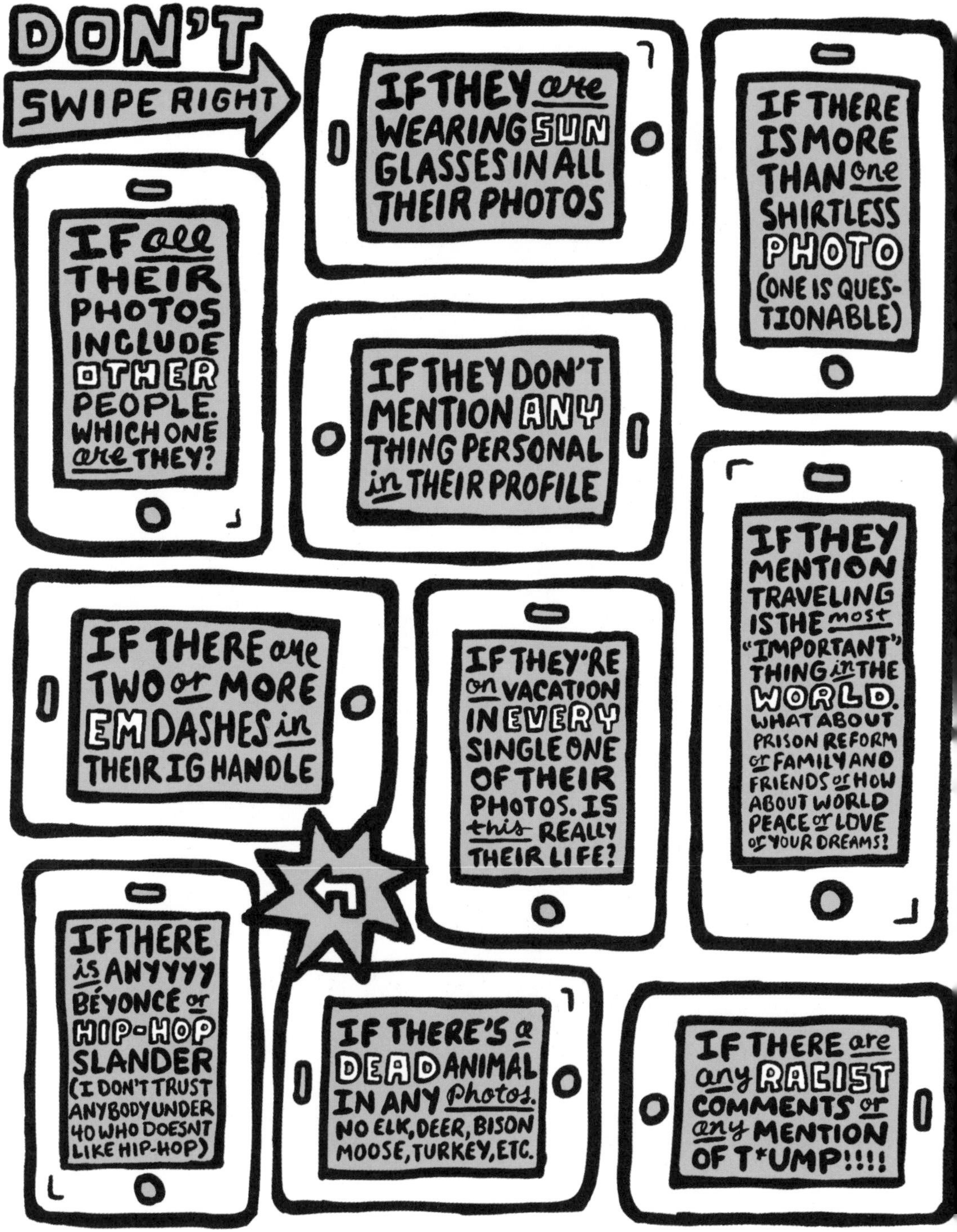

DON'T SWIPE RIGHT
IF THEY are WEARING SUN GLASSES IN ALL THEIR PHOTOS
IF THERE IS MORE THAN one SHIRTLESS PHOTO (ONE IS QUES-TIONABLE)
IF all THEIR PHOTOS INCLUDE OTHER PEOPLE. WHICH ONE are THEY?
IF THEY DON'T MENTION ANY THING PERSONAL in THEIR PROFILE
IF THEY MENTION TRAVELING IS THE most "IMPORTANT" THING in THE WORLD. WHAT ABOUT PRISON REFORM or FAMILY AND FRIENDS or HOW ABOUT WORLD PEACE or LOVE or YOUR DREAMS!
IF THERE are TWO or MORE EM DASHES in THEIR IG HANDLE
IF THEY'RE on VACATION IN EVERY SINGLE ONE OF THEIR PHOTOS. IS this REALLY THEIR LIFE?
IF THERE is ANYYYY BÉYONCE or HIP-HOP SLANDER (I DON'T TRUST ANYBODY UNDER 40 WHO DOESNT LIKE HIP-HOP)
IF THERE'S a DEAD ANIMAL IN ANY Photos. NO ELK, DEER, BISON MOOSE, TURKEY, ETC.
IF THERE are any RACIST COMMENTS or any MENTION OF T*UMP!!!!

JANUARY 18

REGRETS. ALL THIS HAS MADE ME THINK **A LOT** ABOUT MY LAST EX FROM A COUPLE YEARS. MY BIGGEST REGRET WAS AT THE END, WHEN I DIDN'T TELL HER THE THINGS THAT **REALLY** MATTERED, WHEN SHE STOOD IN MY KITCHEN AND WE CRIED AND SAID OUR GOODBYES. I STRUGGLED FOR A LONG TIME AFTERWARDS, WISHING I WAS A BETTER PARTNER TO HER, WISHING I HAD SHARED MORE OF **MY** HEART WITH HER. YOU KNOW THAT SAYING, "YOU MISS 100% OF THE SHOTS YOU DON'T TAKE." ANYWAY, I KNOW NOW THAT SHE **WASN'T** RIGHT, BUT I PROMISED MYSELF THAT I WOULD NEVER AGAIN LET SOMEONE GO WITHOUT A FIGHT. AND HERE I AM WITH ANOTHER **SAD** END, AND I CAN'T HELP BUT WONDER: DID I DO IT AGAIN? MAN, EVERYONE WANTS TO MAKE "FEELINGS" THEIR BRAND ON SOCIAL MEDIA, BUT HOW ARE WE ACTIVELY WORKING ON OUR MENTAL **HEALTH** SO WE CAN BE A MORE SELF-REALIZED PEOPLE AND NOT PUSH OUR ISSUES ON TO OUR LOVERS? AND IN SELF HYPOCRISY TODAY: I'M THINKING ABOUT CALLING AIMÉE BECAUSE I MISS HER AND I WOULD LIKE TO KNOW IF SHE **FEELS** THE SAME WAY.

REALTHINGS

The lovers of my past have moved on to real
things: real experiences and real emotions
and real relationships and real love and real
marriages and sometimes real children. They
show me their real lives and their real smiles
and their real happiness in their real Instagram
photos. I scroll past them and I glance and I sigh
and I yawn and sometimes I roll my eyes and
sometimes I remember what their hair smelled
like. I don't have real relationships with them
anymore, and I'm not sure if I had real relationships with them back then. I do have real
memories, and real laughter, and real mistakes,
and sometimes real regrets about not giving
my real self over to them. But I've realized that
regrets aren't real when you're just picking and

choosing from your life's highlight reel. I don't need to go reeling on that "'Frank Sinatra, she shot me down' so let's go take some shots and forget about everything" kinda trip. That's not really "keeping it real" when the reality is that these experiences all helped me heal. Like all relationships, some of them were the real deal, and some of them I wanted to forget about real fast. So, I write to remind myself that what happened was really real. Now I'm left here scrolling past their real lives in real time, wondering what it means to find something real again.

RANDOM DATING APP BIOS I FOUND

"I'M DRUNK. LIKE RIGHT now. NOT ALWAYS. BUT NOW I am DRUNK."

"I'M FLUENT in FUCK BOI. DON'T TRY it."

"I'M A TOTAL CARRIE. I KNOW EVERY GIRL says THAT. I'M ACTUALLY A MIX of ALL OF THEM. CALL ME 'CHARMANTHANDACAR.'"

"YOU CAN BLOCK ME ON INSTAGRAM BUT you CAN'T UNLICK MY ASS."

"YOU BETTER NOT BE ONE OF THOSE FUCKING PEOPLE who CLAPS WHEN the PLANE LANDS."

"PLEASE DON'T BE BROKE."

"DON'T TALK to ME ABOUT THINGS THAT ARE TRENDING ON TWITTER."

"I ACTUALLY WANT to MEET SOMEONE IN REAL LIFE LOL DON'T JUDGE ME."

"I DON'T KNOW WHAT YOU are LOOKING for BUT I CAN'T FIT IT in THIS BIO."

"I WILL SWIPE LEFT on YOUR ASS WHILE I STEADY COUNT MY MONEY."

"I'VE FARTED in THE SAME ROOM as BEYONCÉ."

"I'M 5'9" so EMOTIONAL SHORTIES NEED NOT APPLY PLEASE."

"WE ALL HAVE a STORY BLAH BLAH BLAH."

"HOW CAN I CONTINUE my LONG SEARCH FOR HUMAN CONNECTION WHILE SIMULTANEOUSLY MAINTAIN the LOWEST POSSIBLE LEVEL OF EMOTIONAL INTIMACY with YOU."

"WINE IS BAD for ME BUT GOOD FOR YOU."

"KNOW HOW to TALK ABOUT ART SHIT."

CHAPTER 11
BARGAINING

I got on the phone and told her this NYC shit ain't shit, and I'd move back to Paris for a chance to fall in love with her one more time. She thought I was talking shit, so she smiled and said it's probably a bad time. But I was on my Ethan Hawke *Before Sunset* shit, ready to fight for our love and leave the life I knew behind. We were talking on FaceTime, I was six hours behind, and I could see the Parisian sunset fade off her face, knowing it was probably my last time. After the most romantic summer I'll always remember, the only thing separating us was an ocean separating us. I thought I was fighting for the love of my life when she told me she already met someone else and she was ready to move on with her life. I said "You know, if we never broke up and I stayed in your city, we'd already be living together with a cute little puppy." She said "Yeah and his name would be Croissant. A little baby Croissant." Sometimes I wish I could miss her without it meaning everything. Sometimes I think of that Bob Dylan line, "I give her my heart, but she wanted my soul" because I guess what I had wasn't enough for her heart to be full. Sometimes Paris calls on me, my phone rings and I wonder if it's her. My mind rings back to the love we so easily let go. Sometimes I wonder if ending it prematurely was the wrong move, because you never know what someone could have really meant to you unless you made a real move. And I can still hear those Italian sirens off in the distance the last time I saw her. I can still smell the cold wet streets when I asked her why she was being distant. I can still feel her hand move away from mine at a moment's instant. I can still see her tears and makeup smeared all over my long white shirt. I can still remember how I felt so alone in Rome on New Year's Eve after neither of us tried to make it work. Because after all the hangovers, and the hanging on to something that doesn't exist, it's so hard to come to grips with the fact that I'll never hang out with her again for as long as I exist.

SOMETIMES WEARENT THERIGHT PEOPLETO THERIGHT PEOPLEAT THERIGHT TIMES

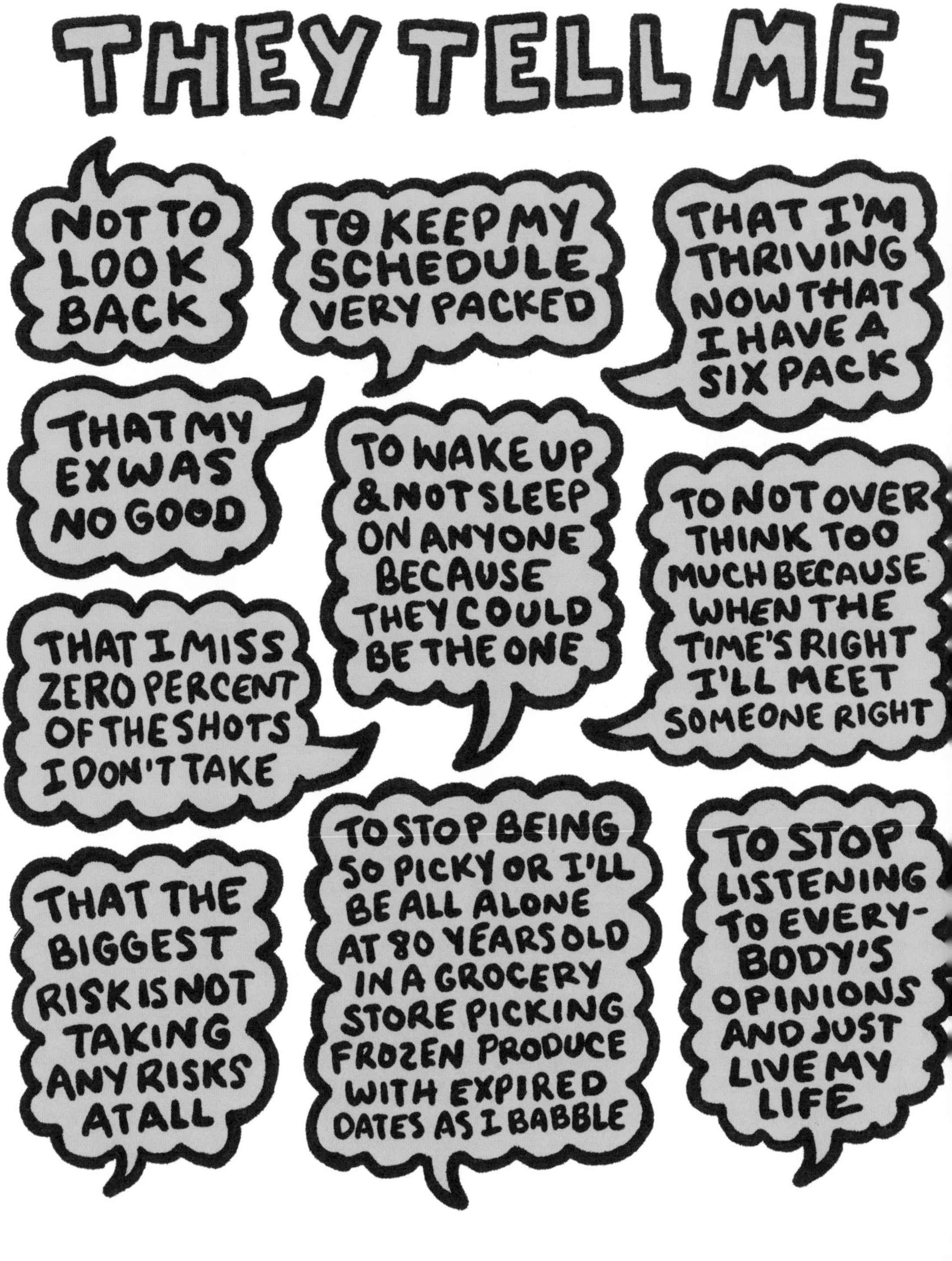
THEY TELL ME
NOT TO LOOK BACK
TO KEEP MY SCHEDULE VERY PACKED
THAT I'M THRIVING NOW THAT I HAVE A SIX PACK
THAT MY EX WAS NO GOOD
TO WAKE UP & NOT SLEEP ON ANYONE BECAUSE THEY COULD BE THE ONE
TO NOT OVER THINK TOO MUCH BECAUSE WHEN THE TIME'S RIGHT I'LL MEET SOMEONE RIGHT
THAT I MISS ZERO PERCENT OF THE SHOTS I DON'T TAKE
THAT THE BIGGEST RISK IS NOT TAKING ANY RISKS AT ALL
TO STOP BEING SO PICKY OR I'LL BE ALL ALONE AT 80 YEARS OLD IN A GROCERY STORE PICKING FROZEN PRODUCE WITH EXPIRED DATES AS I BABBLE
TO STOP LISTENING TO EVERY-BODY'S OPINIONS AND JUST LIVE MY LIFE

JANUARY 25

I'VE BEEN READING bell hooks 'ALL ABOUT LOVE' BECAUSE I FEEL SO SAD THAT I CAN'T IMAGINE HAVING ANYMORE LOVE TO OFFER IN THIS WORLD. REJECTION IS SO HARD. I'M HAPPY I TRIED TO FIGHT FOR HER, EVEN IF IT WAS TOO LATE... BUT **NOW** I FEEL SO UTTERLY TERRIBLE. AND WHAT BOTHERS ME THE MOST IS THAT THIS ISN'T AN UNFAMILIAR FEELING. I HAVE A HISTORY OF GASLIGHTING MY BRAIN WHEN IT COMES TO **PAST** RELATIONSHIPS, ESPECIALLY IF IT WAS A MUTUAL BREAKUP. I ROMANTICIZE THEM, I QUESTION WHY IT ENDED, I FORGET HOW I FELT AT THE END, I DOUBT MY DECISIONS. I WANT TO BE SINCERE WITH MYSELF ABOUT WHAT IS RIGHT FOR ME, BUT MY ATTACHMENT ISSUES ARE SO REAL. ANYWAY, I REALLY THOUGHT SHE'D FEEL THE SAME WAY. I **CAN'T** BELIEVE SHE'S SEEING SOMEONE ALREADY. I MISS HER. IT'S NOT EVERY DAY YOU OFFER TO MOVE COUNTRIES FOR SOMEONE. HOW COULD I EXPECT THAT PROPOSITION TO REALLY WORK ANYWAY? I FEEL SO LOST, I'M CALLING **MY** THERAPIST.

DON'T MISS OUT

You never really know if you're gonna miss out on someone when you let someone go. They could be the person who means the whole wide world to you. They could be the person who turns this whole thing around for you. I mean, they could mean everything. They could do so many meaningful things. They could be the means to this whole big beautiful thing. If you don't give it a chance to grow, then how will you ever know? How will you ever get that second home in that cute little postcard town as your kids play on the playground so innocent and proud? How will your mother-in-law ever make pies in that kitchen as cutie-pies walk around holding hands with real possibility in their eyes? Because once your lover is gone, your pens will write different songs.

No more sharing stories. No more Instagram stories. Just two people who never reached the highest story. And while it's easy to romanticize our stories, sometimes the ones we lose stay with us like family stories handed down, like wrinkles in my hands, we use our memories to feel something again. They are mine. They are yours. They are ours to tell. Another failed relationship is gone until enough days, months, and years go by until I'm confident and sure. Like I haven't hurt and been hurt before. Like I haven't been shaken to my core. Like I'm still a wide-eyed kid moving to NYC at 24. But I guess that's how the story goes, it's just another happy story that will never be told.

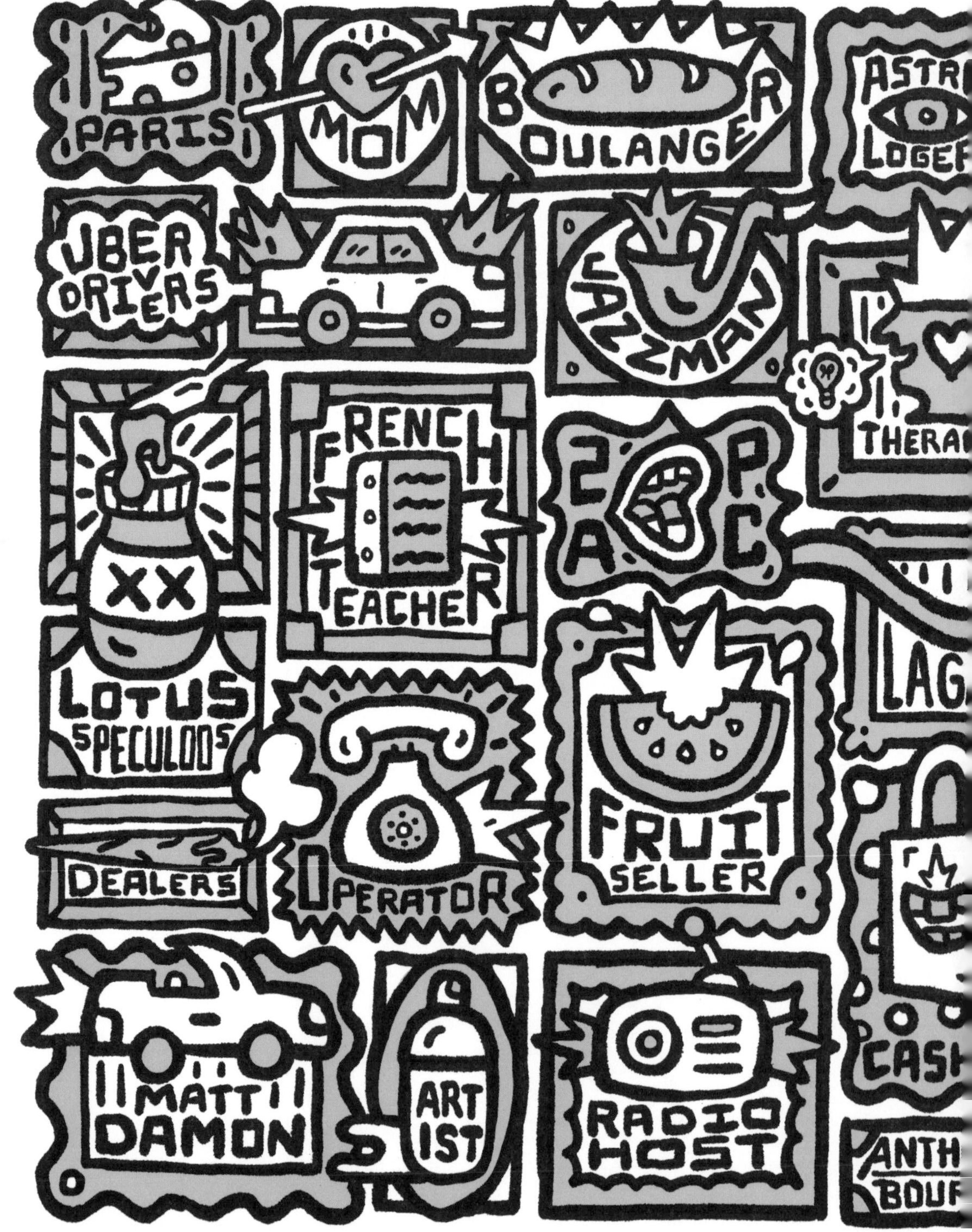
PARIS
MOM
BOULANGER
ASTR
LOGE
UBER DRIVERS
JAZZMAN
THERA
2 A P.C.
FRENCH TEACHER
XX
LOTUS
SPECULOOS
LAG
DEALERS
OPERATOR
FRUIT SELLER
CAS
MATT DAMON
ARTIST
RADIO HOST
ANTH
BOU

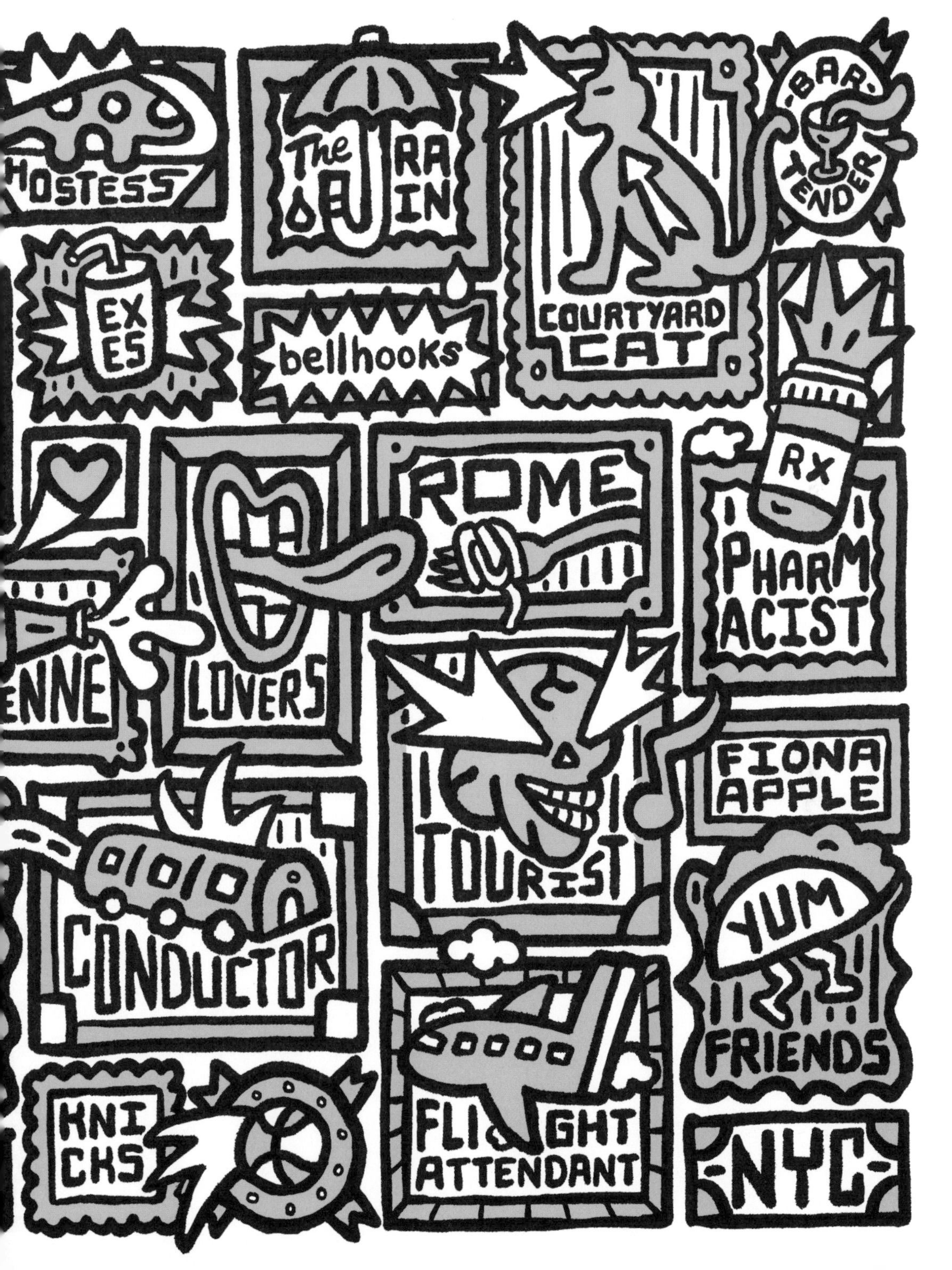

HOSTESS
The RAIN
COURTYARD CAT
BAR-TENDER
EXES
bellhooks
ENNE
LOVERS
ROME
RX
PHARMACIST
TOURIST
FIONA APPLE
CONDUCTOR
YUM
FRIENDS
KNICKS
FLIGHT ATTENDANT
NYC

CHAPTER 12
DEPRESSION

Why do we run up debts on people's hearts when we don't pay the balance on them when we break them? Breaking up is hard enough, but when I found out that she *may* have cheated on me, when the guy she was seeing literally told me, it made my heart fall so fast from the sky that the pressure had me breaking apart. I heard this nonsense, I tried to make it make sense, I lost my two cents, I drank too many drinks, and wrote two intense emails to my therapist like I was 2Pac in his prime. Aimée said it didn't happen. She said I didn't know the who, what, when. She said it was all a big misunderstanding. But after we got off the phone, I continued spiraling. I wanna believe her, and I'm thankful for her words, but there are no words to describe how emotionally triggering this is for someone like myself who can feel so alone in the world. Even the idea of infidelity made me feel like I'm not enough. It made me so ashamed that I shared my heart with someone who could have been insensitive about the way I hurt. I remembered just months ago how happy I felt as we were carving pumpkins at my apartment. I thought it was the beginning of a real future we were carving out together. Now I felt like my heart was just an empty apartment, and every year there's a different tenant. We all gotta pay our dues, but I kept writing checks that my heart couldn't deposit. I kept replaying past conversations, knowing the story would never amount to anything. I kept looking for clues to understand the truth. I kept seeing my rose-colored Parisian glasses fade to dark Roman hues. I kept trying to give myself the benefit of the doubt, the little boy inside me who still can't understand why his parents were so hurt. I kept doubting whether I was benefiting from all that whisky I was drinking to drown out those thoughts. I kept running the memories through my head so much, that I had to run an hour a day to try to outrun the pain. My friends texted me, "Tim, you're not to blame, your values weren't aligned anyway, you both ran away from something that wasn't good enough to stay." But the tears ran down my face so fast, because I couldn't imagine what a future looked like without the weight of my past. I was crying in a bathroom stall because I was so depressed. I was crying because the person I loved loves someone else. I was crying because I stalled the trauma I never worked on after all the years. I was crying because it all just became way too much. I called my mom and broke down because I was breaking apart, and she said, "Baby, you're the best person I know, you'll find someone who will love all of your Timothy heart." Sometimes nothing works, not even work, not working out for my health, not best friends, not Instagram quotes reminding me to be my best self. Sometimes we need loyalty and safety above everything else. Sometimes we have to ask for help. Sometimes we're not the right people to the right people at the right times, and I gotta feel all these painful feelings to feel alive.

FIND YOUR FEELINGS & LET THEM KILL YOU

Six TOPICS I GOOGLE WHEN I'M SAD

WHY AM I
...ALWAYS TIRED
...ALWAYS COLD
...ALWAYS GASSY
...PEEING SO MUCH

WHY ARE MEN
...PAINTING NAILS
...TALLER
...WEARING PEARLS
...LUNATICS

WHY ARE CANCERS
...SO SAD
...SO ANNOYING
...ALWAYS SINGLE
...OBSESSED

WHY DO I
...FEEL NAUSEOUS
...OWE TAXES
...SWEAT AT NIGHT
...HAVE DIARRHEA

WHY DID
...I GET MARRIED
...GOD CREATE US
...I WAKE UP
...WILL SLAP CHRIS

WHY DOES EARTH
...HAVE SEASONS
...HAVE LAYERS
...SPIN ON ITS AXIS
...REVOLVE 'ROUND ME

FEBRUARY 2

THESE ARE MY CURRENT FEARS:

THAT IT TAKES 12 TO 15 MONTHS SCIENTIFICALLY TO GET OVER A SERIOUS RELATIONSHIP. (WTF!)

THAT THE PEOPLE WE **LOVE** HAVE DIRECT ACCESS TO OUR PAIN, TRAUMA, AND INSECURITIES.

THAT **THE** LYRICS TO THE SONG "YOU OUGHTA KNOW" BY ALANIS MORISSETTE WILL BE THE EPITAPH ON MY TOMBSTONE. AMOUR **FOU**?

THAT **MY** THERAPIST WILL NEVER STOP ROLLING HIS EYES AT ME EVERY TIME I SAY "I'LL NEVER FIND REAL LOVE WITH ANYBODY EVER."

THAT THE LAST FEAR IS **TRUE**. (IT IS. RIGHT?)

THAT MY SPOTIFY PLAYLISTS **ARE** ONLY GREAT WHEN I'M HEARTBROKEN. (MY LATEST ONE IS PURE FIREEEE. I FORGOT ABOUT "CIGARETTES AFTER SEX"!)

THAT JOHNNY THUNDERS WAS RIGHT WHEN HE SANG, "YOU CAN'T PUT YOUR ARM AROUND A MEMORY. DON'T TRY." DAMN.

THAT THIS UNBEARABLE SHAME **AND** SELF-LOATHING WILL WEIGH ON ME FOREVER.

THAT I'LL NEVER BE ABLE TO GO BACK TO PARIS BECAUSE IT'S COMPLETELY CONTAMINATED NOW. AND **ROME?** I CAN'T IMAGINE COMING BACK.

THAT I WILL SPEND THE REST OF **MY** LIFE IN ROME EATING THE WORLD'S GREATEST FOOD, WHICH I'LL NEVER BE ABLE TO ENJOY. A **LITTLE** TASTE OF HELL, I GUESS.

TOUGH ACT TO FOLLOW

"She's a tough act to follow." That's what my boy William said to me while I was following whisky after whisky in some Roman dive bar at 2 AM, trying to tough out the pain. What a comment. What a slap in my face. Honestly, I wanted to punch him right in the fucking face. "How about, I'm a tough act to follow!" I drunkenly yelled down the bar at a bunch of Italian tough guys who looked at me in confusion. "How about I'm a tough act to follow!" I yelled like a tough guy at Instagram as I unfollowed Aimée and all her friends because, hey, why not make another bad decision? So, this is how you break up: take zero intuition, cut half the pain, add a little whisky, subtract your fate, multiply that by all the times you took the empty bait and made dumb mistakes, and divide that by the fact that two halves won't make you whole or truly happy like you see in the movies. When you break up, don't glue the pieces back together. Let them be loose, let them find their legs and walk away with dignity. Breaking up is the easy stuff, it's finding out about the rough stuff like they didn't have my best interests at heart, that they weren't sensitive about how I hurt, that they didn't love me the way I deserved. Breaking up is like bruising my knee when I'm drunk. I can't feel it right away, but eventually I'll be crying at a shitty bar in Rome about how I unfollowed my ex because she wasn't the one. No, breaking up isn't what breaks me up, it's all that other stuff that eventually breaks my heart. It's a tough act to follow, not knowing how to restart.

FEBRUARY 9

IN 'ALL ABOUT LOVE,' bell WRITES, "MOST OF US PREFER TO HAVE A PARTNER WHO IS LACKING THAN NO PARTNER AT ALL. WHAT BECOMES APPARENT IS THAT WE MAY BE MORE INTERESTED IN FINDING A PARTNER THAN IN KNOWING LOVE." I JUST BROKE DOWN CRYING. HOW CAN I TRULY KNOW LOVE WHEN I GREW UP SEEING MY MOTHER AND STEPDAD CONSTANTLY FIGHTING, DEVOID OF ANY AFFECTION? WHEN I'M NOT SABOTAGING OR RUNNING AWAY FROM PARTNERS WHO ARE GOOD FOR ME, I'M FALLING IN LOVE WITH ONES WHO ARE JUST SO UNMISTAKABLY NOT RIGHT. MY THERAPIST SAYS I HAVE AN ATTACHMENT DISORDER AND SOMETHING CALLED "ABANDONMENT DEPRESSION." IT WAS WRITTEN THAT I SHOULD BE LOYAL TO THE NIGHTMARE OF MY CHOICE. FUCK THAT. I KEEP ASKING MYSELF: HOW DO I REFRAME THE DIALOGUE I AM HAVING WITH MYSELF WHEN I AM GOING THROUGH DEPRESSION AND HEARTBREAK? INSTEAD OF ASKING "WHY CAN'T I BE HAPPY?" I WISH TO SAY "IT'S OKAY TO FEEL LIKE THIS." I REALLY DO.

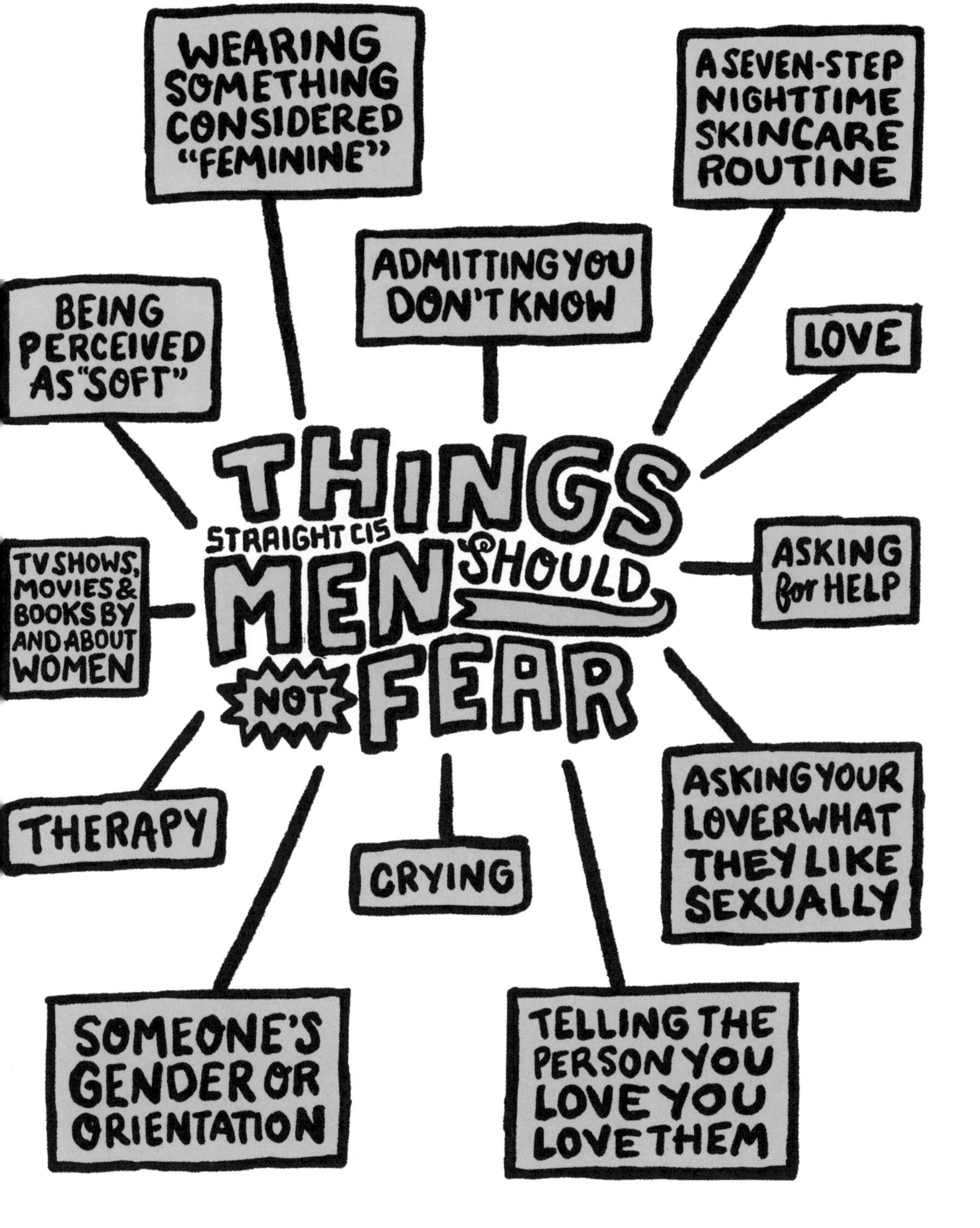
THINGS STRAIGHT CIS MEN SHOULD NOT FEAR
WEARING SOMETHING CONSIDERED "FEMININE"
A SEVEN-STEP NIGHTTIME SKINCARE ROUTINE
ADMITTING YOU DON'T KNOW
BEING PERCEIVED AS "SOFT"
LOVE
ASKING for HELP
TV SHOWS, MOVIES & BOOKS BY AND ABOUT WOMEN
THERAPY
CRYING
ASKING YOUR LOVER WHAT THEY LIKE SEXUALLY
SOMEONE'S GENDER OR ORIENTATION
TELLING THE PERSON YOU LOVE YOU LOVE THEM

CHAPTER 13
RECONSTRUCTION

Doctors say we develop strategies for dealing with abandonment and rejection by the time we're 18 months old, about the age I was when my father left town with another girl. Like many, the love I desired from a father was misplaced. My first stepdad would throw me against the wall and scream in my face until the tears ran down my face. I can still smell his cigarette and coffee breath as his bearded face became so red. I was six, seven, eight years old, and I didn't understand why this new dad would get so mad. I didn't understand why he didn't act like a "dad." The screaming bouts between him and my mom got worse, and so did the drugs in the house, the anxiety around money, and all the confusion I felt around something that I thought was my fault. Seeing two adults in pain—hurting each other, avoiding each other, never showing love or real communication—stayed with me as an adult. It made me never wanna open up my heart. Instead of seeing love as a beautiful bond that can lead to incredible experiences and growth, I began to associate a relationship as a shortcoming filled with inevitable heartache and pain. I also saw it as something a "man" was too busy and proud for. I'd hold myself back for fear that love would not work out, putting up many walls in the process, and often times, never truly letting go. The PTSD attachment disorder I've developed is the root of the pain I feel when I feel betrayed, like an old athletic injury that still remains. Broken boys become broken men, and it took me a long time to admit that I am ill-equipped at managing the emotional capacity I need to become a more self-realized man. My therapist repeatedly tells me that I am "lovable and worthy of love," because he knows that every time I hear this line it still feels like the first time I've ever heard it. It helps me to see my own limits. It helps me confront my loneliness with a strategy kit. So, I seek help through therapy, and I share my own story because I want to inspire men to admit that they need help, to be proactive about their insecurities, and to choose

vulnerability over aggression and apathy, be–
cause even I still constantly struggle with toxic
masculinity. I was 35 when I was finally able
to admit that I was physically abused, because
it was my ego that was still severely bruised.
My childhood, with all the love from my wonderful
momma (and 80s Madonna!) mixed with the
family drama and the trauma, has now made me
see the world as a modern antique, because
every word I speak, every breath I breathe, I want
to live my life with sustained intensity. I am
forever hungry, with real desire for accountability
and sincerity. It's a life's work to unlearn the
attitudes I adopted as a kid, to look in the mirror,
to look within, and despite the bad days where
I can't block out the pain in my head, I try to take
care of myself as much as I can.

YOU ARE LOVABLE & YOU ARE WORTHY OF LOVE

FEBRUARY 27

I STARTED TAKING ANTIDEPRESSION MEDICINE. I'VE NEVER TAKEN MEDICATION FOR MENTAL ILLNESS BEFORE, BUT I'M JUST FEELING REALLY DESPAIRED **LATELY** WITH SUCH EXTREME HIGHS AND LOWS. I'VE HAD SUCH A COMPULSIVE CYCLE OF THOUGHTS, AND I'VE BEEN OVERLY OBSESSIVE ABOUT EVERYTHINGGG. I HAVEN'T **BEEN** SLEEPING, I'M HAVING PANIC ATTACKS, AND I'M CRYING A LOT. IT JUST HASN'T GOTTEN BETTER DESPITE HAVING THE OCCASIONAL GOOD DAY, EXERCISING REGULARLY, AND TRYING TO "PUSH THROUGH." IT'S NOT HARD FOR **ME** TO ADMIT I NEED HELP, AND I DON'T FEEL ASHAMED ABOUT MEDICATION, BUT I'VE HEARD SUCH A MIXED BAG OF NEGATIVE AND POSITIVE THINGS, SO I HAVE MY RESERVATIONS. AT FIRST, I STRUGGLED WITH A LITTLE BIT OF **SHAME**, BUT DESPITE MY SADNESS RIGHT NOW, I DO HAVE PRIDE IN KNOWING THAT I'M BEING PROACTIVE **ABOUT** MY MENTAL HEALTH. I'M TRYING.

FATHER TIME

Seven years ago, I met my biological father for the first time in my life. I never talked to him before that, never got advice. I never saw a photo of the man, never got a lesson on how to be a "man." The day after meeting him, I was shaving in my hotel suite, I looked in the mirror and saw his teeth. I saw his round cheeks. I saw his light eyes. I saw his thinning hair. I saw his broad shoulders. I felt the weight I had been carrying on my shoulders for so long suddenly disappear. Up until that moment, I always liked not seeing where my features came from. I liked not seeing the person who ran away from me and my mom. But after that, I became so much more thankful for who I am. I grew to love the place that I'm from. I learned to enjoy the process as I strive to constantly be in a state of becoming. As I get older, I try to be more forgiving to this man who I was never very fond of. I try to be more patient and more vulnerable. I try to always be sensitive to this world. There are times when I'm feeling down and I'll text my mom. I'll watch those three dots bounce around, and I'm so thankful for her because she's always been around. She always took me to see the Christmas lights downtown. And I ask myself, Will I regret not being around now? Do I *really* make time for those who hold me down? Should I go down and see her more? When will all the "more" matter more? When will I stop treating it like a chore? So, I tear up because one day I won't see those dots pop back up because I know she'll be gone.

TOXIC

HE'S a TOXIC man FULL of TOXIC MASCULINITY. HE'S TOO "MANLY" TO LOOK AT HIS SEXUALITY.

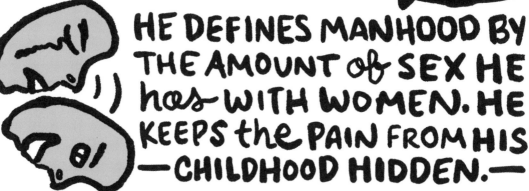

HE DEFINES MANHOOD BY THE AMOUNT of SEX HE has WITH WOMEN. HE KEEPS the PAIN FROM HIS —CHILDHOOD HIDDEN.—

HE CALLS WOMEN "HOES" and "BITCHES". HE MAKES FUN OF OTHERS for BEING THEMSELVES BECAUSE HE DOESNT have THE COURAGE.

HE'S ANOTHER STRAIGHT DUDE who GREW UP WITH a CROOKED LINEAGE. HIS DAD WOULD STRAIGHT UP BEAT HIS ASS and CALL HIM "DAMAGED."

HE is SCARED STRAIGHT BY HIS OWN POSSIBILITIES. HE HOOKED UP with A BOY BUT if ANYONE FOUND OUT HE'D LOSE his FAMILY.

HE IS A TOXIC MAN full of TOXIC MASCULINITY. HE INTOXICATES HIMSELF SO HE CAN AVOID his OWN VULNERABILITY.

CHAPTER 14
REFLECTION

I'm never really prepared for the idea that a relationship can fail when everything is going so well in the beginning. It's like flying first class on an airplane so I can lie down and drink champagne. Yeah I paid extra for a more comfortable ride, but will it really matter when it crashes down? Please, let me be in style during my emotional disaster. You gotta wonder, maybe a 75-ton chunk of machinery isn't supposed to fly in the sky. Maybe only birds are supposed to perform that wonder. I guess the same could be said for traditional romantic relationships. Maybe they aren't supposed to fly either? We fall in love, get married, have a child, fake a smile, it's all such a 1950s lifestyle. However, Cupid, with his strange baby wings and gold-tipped arrows, happens to be flying around everywhere shooting poor souls like me in the heart. When I spend time with someone I love, my heart does sorta pay into an at-risk investment for a more comfortable ride at this life. And when I lose them, particularly when they leave me, I'm left with all these feelings that I can no longer cash in on. It's like having currency for a casino that is no longer around. It's a sobering feeling, sitting there with all my expired chips, finally able to admit that I was playing to win. No, I wasn't playing for the experience of the game. I was playing for forever plus a surname. I can hear my banker remind me to not pull my money out when the market gets volatile, so I can't help but ask: do I do this every time I approach a relationship obstacle? People change, people want different things, people wanna grow apart, people grow tired of the ordinary, and people yearn for other people. I guess it pays to forget that people usually hurt other people when the chance of finding real love wipes away all the old debts.

PEOPLECHANGE,
PEOPLEWANT
VERYDIFFERENT
THINGS,PEOPLE
WANNAGROW
APART,PEOPLE
GROWTIREDOF
THEORDINARY,
PEOPLEYEARN
FORMOREPEOPLE

LIFE PROCESS
& PERSPECTIVE & ACCEPTANCE

MY HAIR

LETTING go

MY FRIENDS GETTING MARRIED

FINDING MYSELF

THERAPY

LOSING MYSELF

ME, CARING ABOUT PEOPLE

LEARN-ING about my PRIVILEGES & TAKING ACTION

PEOPLE BEING PUNISHED for WHO THEY ARE

REMEMBERING PEOPLE with BIG FOLLOWINGS on SOCIAL are NOT NECESSARILY:

RICH

HAPPY

THE BEST

MAKING ANY THING THAT IS MEANINGFUL

MARCH 24

"WE GOT THIS, KIDDO." THAT'S WHAT **MY** THERAPIST TEXTED ME TODAY AS THE FLIGHT ATTENDANT WAS GOING THROUGH THE SAFETY PROCEDURES BEFORE MY FLIGHT **BACK** TO NYC. IT MADE ME ASK, HOW SAFE AM I FROM MYSELF? AS I STRUGGLE WITH WHAT IT MEANS TO HAVE ABANDONMENT DEPRESSION AND AN ATTACHMENT DISORDER, PUTTING THESE KINDS OF LABELS ON THE WAYS I FEEL **HELPS** ME PROCESS EVERYTHING SO MUCH BETTER. THE LOSS OF A RELATIONSHIP CAN FEEL MUCH MORE SIGNIFICANT FOR ME **THAN** IT DOES FOR OTHER FOLKS. BUT MY THERAPIST KEEPS REMINDING ME THAT I DON'T HAVE TO APOLOGIZE OR BE ASHAMED FOR IT. HE REMINDS ME DAILY THAT I AM LOVABLE AND WORTHY OF **LOVE**. I'M LEARNING TO ACCEPT THAT ABOUT MYSELF. IT'S BEEN A 12-YEAR RELATIONSHIP ON AND OFF SINCE I WAS IN COLLEGE, AND HE REALLY IS MY ROBIN WILLIAMS IN 'GOOD WILL HUNTING'. I FUCKING LOVE THIS MAN SO MUCH. **WE** GOT THIS.

IT'S OKAY TO NOT BE OKAY

We never met IRL, but I took a one-hour plane ride to see someone who wasn't the one because I was feeling lonely and solo and YOLO, and if I was being real, I would say those pics she sent me were too damn good to say no to. After an hour of awkward moments, there was this one moment where she put on her favorite Drake track, and she rapped real loud to that part where he raps "I might talk that real if you ask me what I care about, rap and bitches, rappin' bitches, bitches and rappin'." And I guess it all switches, one moment we're strangers and another she's real and we're distracting ourselves from everything in our lives that's too real. No heart-to-hearts, no questions like "What fills up your heart?", no one there to pay the balance on our broken hearts. She turned my pain into my favorite lyric, she gave me lyrical moments despite my inner critic. Lying in bed at 2 AM sharing our favorite concert moments, she got all serious when she lip-synced her favorite Frank Ocean lyric. And even tho I knew this moment wouldn't last much longer because she and I were like two oceans separated by water, just two people using each other so that we were no longer drowning forever, I'm so thankful for our time together. As I write this with tears in my eyes, I'm starting to feel so fucking alive. I'm feeling like it's okay to not be okay, and that feels pretty great for me today.

DID YOU ACCEPT it?

"MY LIFE CHANGED when I LEARNED to FORGIVE THOSE who HURT ME, out LOUD and SPECIFIC ABOUT WHAT HURT. IT RE-ROUTES MY BRAIN to LIVE with FORGIVENESS."

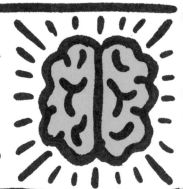

"IT TOOK me 10 YEARS to WRITE ABOUT MY HEARTACHE and ONCE I did IT LIFTED a VERY HEAVY WEIGHT off ME. I WISH I FOUND the WORDS EARLIER."

"I WAKE UP with HOPE that SOMEONE WILL SHOW ME that LOVE is ENOUGH. MAYBE THAT will BE ME."

"I'M GRATEFUL to EXPERIENCE THIS HEARTBREAK, as i SHED a NEW SKIN."

"WENT THROUGH A LOT WITH SOMEONE I *was* CONVINCED WAS MY PERSON. THEY WERE NOT. BUT *all* THE WORK I'VE DONE SINCE THEM, THE NEXT PERSON I SPEND *my* TIME WITH *is* GETTING AN UPGRADE."

NOT *all* LOVE STORIES WORTH TELLING HAVE *to* BE EPIC. THE FLEETING LOVES, UNREQUITED LOVES & THE HEART BROKEN NEED TO BE TOLD *so* WE CAN HEAL."

"YOU CAN FEEL *so* ALONE BUT THEN REALIZE HOW MANY SONGS, POEMS, *and* ART ARE ABOUT THE SAME THING YOU ARE FEELING. *It's* GREAT."

I'M BETTER FOR HAVING HAD THE HEART BREAK & LOVE."

CHAPTER 15

ACCEPTANCE

I sat at my computer for an hour trying to craft a five-sentence note to her that was light but meaningful, cute but serious, straightforward but vague. So many questions unanswered. So much closure I wanted. So much confusion inside. So much I wanted to talk about and understand why. So many messy feelings I couldn't transcribe. The last time Aimée and I FaceTimed, she said I could have fought for her when we ended things back on New Year's Eve, but now I know I didn't do that because I knew she wasn't right for me. So many red flags I didn't see. So much incompatibility. So many times I feel like she didn't value all the beautiful messy things that make me "me." Suddenly, everything that happened between us at the end became completely insignificant to me. No longer am I going to play in the deep shadows of hurt, because relationships are impossible to foreshadow. I'd rather believe in my heart. I used to play it cool, I was afraid to act a fool for what I cared about, but no longer will I be ashamed to shoot and miss for the stars.

I will laugh and cry equally because I have to accept myself for what I am: an imperfect human being. And since our breakup, the depression I felt, the wanting to take it all back, the heartache I had for something I didn't deserve, all made me wanna scream my pain out to the world. And like Fiona Apple sang, "It ended bad but I love what we started. . . All the signs said 'stop' but we went on wholehearted." And I do love what we started. And maybe I shouldn't always let my past overlap the present, but I know my existence is the sum of all the memories that mattered. And what matters is that she mattered to me. So, despite all the heartache I've felt inside, I wouldn't trade what we shared because that shit made me feel alive. Besides, I'm more than someone else's memory, so I deleted the note I wrote her so I could begin writing my own story. And that's just the way this story goes, it's just another love story that will never be fully told.

MY ENTIRE
EXISTENCE
IS THE SUM
OF ALL THE
MEMORIES
THAT HAVE
MATTERED

IF WE BREAK UP,
DONT GLUE ALL THE
PIECES BACK TO
GETHER, LET THEM
BE LOOSE, LET THEM
FIND THEIR LEGS &
WALK AWAY WITH
DIGNITY, LET THEM
FILL UP THE EMPTY
HOLE THAT'S DEEP
INSIDE THEIR SOUL.

APRIL 19

I CRIED ON THE PHONE YESTERDAY TO MY MOM. EVERY DAY I HEAL FROM THIS BREAKUP, I JUST COME BACK TO THE CONFUSION, LONELINESS, AND ABUSE I EXPERIENCED AS A KID. AND WHAT'S WILD IS THAT IT TOOK ME MY WHOLE LIFE TO ADMIT THAT I WAS EVEN ABUSED! OUR CONVERSATION WAS HONEST AND HEARTBREAKING AND HEALING. AND I'M STILL GROWING, BUT I STAND HERE ALIVE WITH MY WHOLE BEING, BECAUSE DESPITE ALL THAT HAS HAPPENED THE LAST SEVERAL MONTHS, NONE OF IT ACTUALLY MATTERS. WHAT MATTERS IS NOT LETTING IT HAVE POWER. WHAT MATTERS IS HOW I IDENTIFY WITH IT. WHAT MATTERS IS LETTING THE STREAM OF LOVE RUN THROUGH ME. WHAT MATTERS IS HOW I WORK WITH MY FEARS. BESIDES, THERE'S NO SUCH THING AS BEING "FEARLESS." I NEVER STOP BEING AFRAID, I JUST GET BETTER AT OVERCOMING THE FEAR. I DON'T NEED TO CARRY THIS HEAVY BAG ANY LONGER. I'M PUTTING IT DOWN NOW.

SORRY, MOM

Sorry, mom, still no wife, or a husband either. No grandkids running in your backyard, nobody to take home for Thanksgiving dinner. No one to come home to after a long work trip, nobody there to ask me what we should eat for dinner. No reason other than sometimes things just run their course, or I work too much, or I don't try hard enough to make things work, or I have this deep fear that all relationships will just end in a horrible soul-sucking heartbreaking divorce. Sorry, mom, I know you worked all day on your feet to make ends meet, I know you made all the teacher meet and greets, I know you'd love to see me settle down with someone who meets my needs. Sorry, mom, I know you were pregnant, confused, broke, 21 years old, working at the local gas station when you had me. Sorry, mom, you know I've tried much more, you know I've gotten much better, you know I want those 60 years under my belt like grandma and grandpa. I want to get it together, but just know that I won't settle for someone for the sake of being together, even as you're texting me "Try to remember that you're on the right path no matter the weather." Maybe I have unrealistic expectations, maybe I'll be by myself forever, but whatever happens, just know that I love you, so I'll call you later.

THE ANATOMY

WE WERE TOGETHER for 180 DAYS

SHE LIKED all 81 PHOTOS OF MINE

I LIKED all 24 PHOTOS OF HERS

I READ every TWEET!

I LAUGHED at HER FOR HAVING 3,000 TABS OPENED on HER LAPTOP

SHE LAUGHED at ME FOR SAYING WORDS WEIRDLY

WE SENT COUNTLESS ASTROLOGY MEMES

I MADE HER A LOT of HANDMADE NOTES

SHE SURPRISED ME with a TRIP to DISNEYLAND

I CARRIED HER BED FRAME UP THE STAIRS

WE BINGED WATCHED THREE TV SERIES

SHE CRIED DURING SAD MOVIES & THAT ALLOWED ME to SEE HER

I SAW all the SIGNS

WE STOPPED BEING HONEST all THE TIME

WE ENDED our TIME in AN AIRBNB IN ROME

OF A RELATIONSHIP

I WATCHED EVERY IG STORY of HERS

I OPENED EVERY LINK SHE SENT me

I LIKED every FB PROFILE PIC

WE ate SNAILS ONE TIME

SHE SAID "I LOVE you" FIRST

SHE BEAT me TWICE IN "BABY FOOT"

WE KISSED in 2 COUNTRIES

WE EACH MADE PLAYLISTS

SHE TOOK ME to THE EMERGENCY ROOM

I MADE ROOM for HER TOOTHBRUSH

WE SAW 'ONCE UPON a TIME in HOLLY-WOOD' & I SAW HER in GLASSES for THE FIRST TIME

WE BOTTLED UP TOO MUCH

WE DRANK FROM the WHISKY BOTTLE the NIGHT WE ENDED

I WONDER what I COULD HAVE DONE DIFFERENTLY

I LEARNED WHAT KIND OF PARTNER I NEED in THE END

CHAPTER 16

HOPE

(D)o you have a love story that was never told? Do you ever think of the lonely people, the ones who bend over at night holding themselves alive wondering why they don't have someone to love? Maybe it was you. Maybe it was them. Maybe it died before it ever really began. Maybe you wonder what it could have really been. I write for you today, those who have been pushed away, those who push everyone away, those who don't know what to say or how to say it. I write for those who have given every part of their heart away, those who have shut their hearts off because they can't manage the pain, and those who wanna go back and make a change. I write for the shy, the ill, the ones who are misunderstood, all those giant hearts that aren't being filled. I write for the assholes, douchebags, bitches, the ones who ruin everything they've ever held. I write for the vulnerable, the compassionate, the ones who love so deeply that they can't see the truth ahead. I'm reflecting on my growing pains, for who I was and for who I became, for

who's in my life, for who left, and for those who
said I changed. I'm pondering the things I regret
and the words I can't take back, the memories I
tried to run away from, the times I had my heart
stomped on, and for those I hurt in the long run.
I'm longing for the people I no longer know, for
the places I've always wanted to go, for the cities
I've never seen before. I'm seeing visions of my
past through my mind's holey screen door on a
house I couldn't afford. I'm on the ground floor
opening up drawers of memories that just don't
exist anymore. I'm reminding myself that what
I've done is really real, that all I experienced can't
be taken away from my life's highlight reel. I'm
present to the fact that the lovers of my past were
supposed to be there, and they were supposed
to pass. I believe lovers should protect the hearts
of the ones they once loved long after they've
been apart. I believe the parts of our hearts that
we ignore turn into wild animals who are so
scared of being hurt. I believe breakups involve a
grieving process that we should respect, other–

wise we just use a new one as a quick fix without working on all our shit. I believe a relationship is not a casual endeavor, having a real connection with someone is a rare thing as I get older. I believe it's a privilege to be heartbroken, what a testament to the capacity the heart has to feel so deeply for someone. And I still believe in real, lasting love, because I finally know I can really love. I want that big, bold, corny, urgent, ridiculous, inconvenient Carrie Bradshaw kinda love. A friend recently said to me, "We should not love our partners the way we need to be loved. We should love them the way they need to be loved." How beautiful, I can't wait for that day to come.

THE PEOPLE
OF MY PAST
WERE SUPP
OSED TO BE
THERE AND
THEY WERE
SUPPOSED
TO PASS

JUNE 23

HAPPY BIRTHDAY TO ME! I CAN'T BELIEVE A YEAR AGO I WAS PREPARING TO LEAVE FOR PARIS AND JUST 6 MONTHS AGO I WAS PLANNING MY TRIP TO ROME. WOW. DOES THE PAIN FROM THAT BREAK UP STILL PIERCE ME AT TIMES? YES. BUT MY HEAD IS HIGH NOW. I LEARNED, PERHAPS FOR THE FIRST TIME, WHAT I REALLY WANT AND DO NOT WANT IN A PARTNER. A FRIEND ONCE SAID "RIPE FRUIT FALLS QUICKLY." WELL, I'M SO VERY READY. MY HEART EXPLODES EVERY MORNING I WAKE UP. I HEAR BIRDS CHIRPING. I'VE READ THREE BOOKS RECENTLY INCLUDING 'DEVOTION' BY PATTI SMITH. I'M STILL LEARNING FRANÇAIS WITH SANDRA ON ZOOM (THAT'S DEVOTION!). I MET GRETA GERWIG ON THE STREET. I'VE BOUGHT A LOT OF FLOWERS. I'VE COOKED MORE THAN I EVER HAVE IN MY LIFE. I REWATCHED KEN BURNS'S 20-HOUR JAZZ DOCU-MENTARY THAT I LOVE. I'VE HAD EXTREMELY INTIMATE

CONVERSATIONS WITH **OLD** AND NEW FRIENDS. I DRINK MY TEA SLOWER IN THE MORNING. I'VE FELT MORE CONNECTED TO MY CITY, NEW YORK CITY, **THAN** I HAVE IN MY 17 YEARS SINCE MOVING HERE. PEOPLE COME AND GO LIKE THE SEASONS AND THE SNOW, AND SOMETIMES I'M YEARNING FOR PLACES I NO LONGER KNOW. YES, PARIS WILL ALWAYS EXIST IN MY MIND AS SOME INCREDIBLE MOVIE, BUT **THAT** MOMENT WAS NEVER MEANT TO BE ANYTHING BUT TEMPORARY. I'D RATHER HAVE MY CURRENT REALITY. À **LA** PROCHAINE!

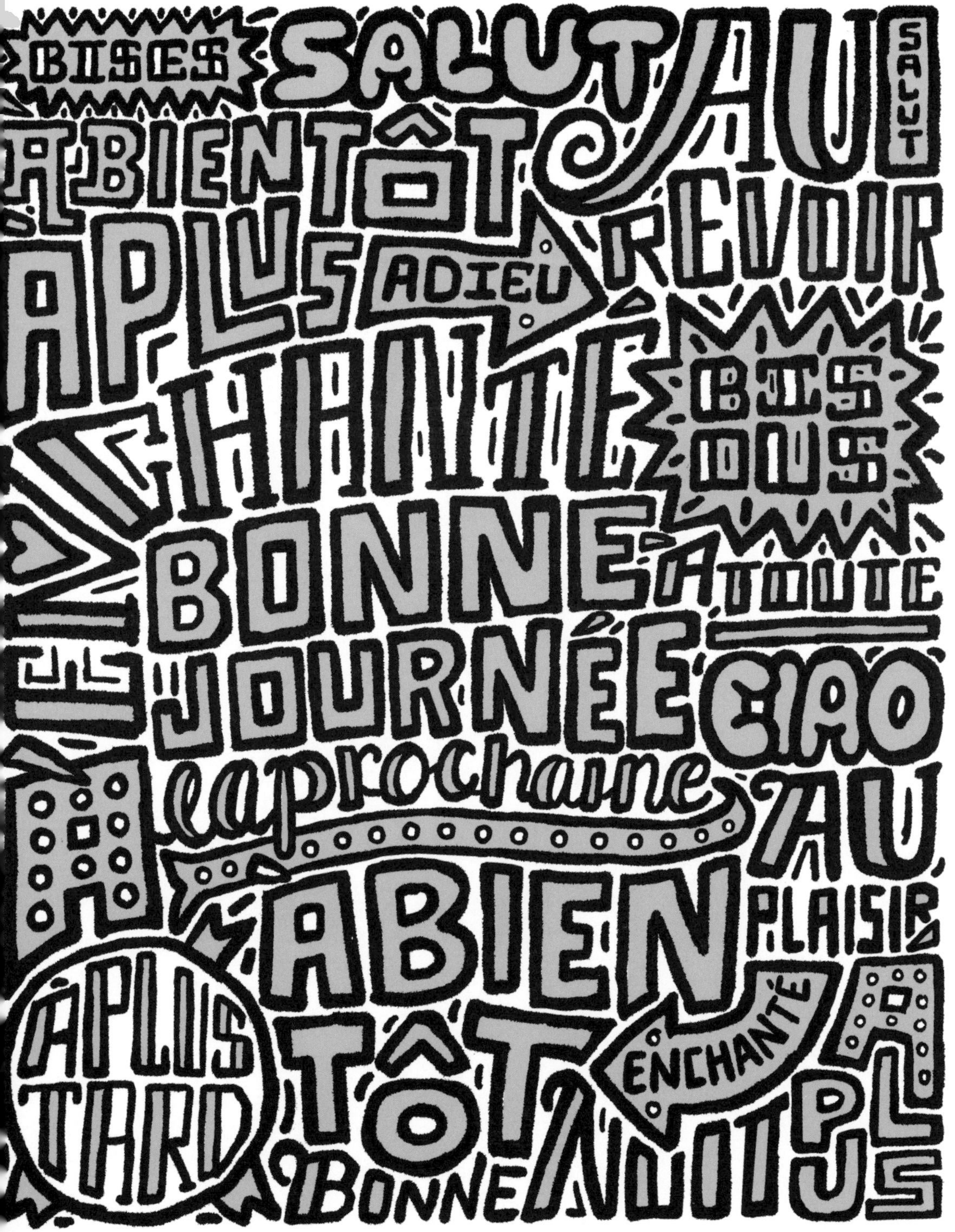

BISES
SALUT
AU REVOIR
SALUT
À BIENTÔT
À PLUS
ADIEU
BISOUS
BONNE JOURNÉE
À TOUTE
CIAO
la prochaine
AU PLAISIR
À BIEN TÔT
À PLUS TARD
ENCHANTÉ
À PLUS
BONNE NUIT

EVERY TIME I
FALL in LOVE
IT'S SUMMER.

I'VE SAID "I LOVE YOU" FIVE TIMES in 20 YEARS of DATING. THAT'S ONCE EVERY FOUR SUMMERS LIKE the WORLD CUP.

IT'S JUST TOO SPECIAL OF AN EVENT TO ME. I GUESS I NEEDED TIME FOR THE QUALIFICATION TOURNAMENTS to BE PLAYED IN-BETWEEN. AND JUST LIKE THAT SOCCER BALL, I HAD TO RUN AFTER LOVE, EVEN if IT WAS ALL WRONG IN THE LONG RUN. ALL I KNOW IS THAT I'M OLD ENOUGH TO KNOW THAT i'll NEVER BE OLD ENOUGH TO KNOW.

EVERY DECISION I MAKE is THE RIGHT DECISION BECAUSE THEY ARE MINE. so, I'LL NEVER KEEP SCORE, BUT I will KEEP ROOTING FOR REAL LOVE.

Acknowledgments
FOREVER, THE END

MOM

TO my LOVELY MOMMA. THANK YOU for YOUR INFECTIOUS SENSE of HUMOR. MOM, YOU WILL ALWAYS BE my "ONE."

PARIS

THANKS to PARIS, of COURSE. YOU STILL LIVE in MY MIND as SOME DREAM. THANKS for NOTHING, ROME (JK).

AGENTS

MANY HEARTS to MY AGENT JESSECA SALKY at SALKY LITERARY MANAGEMENT and TO THE LEGEND CHARLOTTE SHEEDY, who ONCE SAID TO ME "LET'S TALK WHEN you HAVE SOMETHING to SAY." THANK YOU.

FAM

TO my GRANDPARENTS for YOUR GRACIOUSNESS & YOUR CURIOSITY OF TRAVEL that INSPIRED my OWN. TO UNCLE KEV FOR BRINGING so MANY LAUGHS TO MY CHILDHOOD.

THERAPIST

TO MY THERAPIST for LETTING me TURN YOUR OFFICE INTO A POETRY SLAM. TO ANYONE who HELPS men CHOOSE VULNERABILITY OVER APATHY.

TO _my_ BEAUTIFUL FRIENDS (THE OLD, _the_ NEW, _the_ FORMER & THE INTERNET ONES—Y'ALL KNOW _who you_ ARE!). SOME SPECIAL HEARTS _to_ ZACH, JEREMY, DAVE N, WILLIE, JOHNNY, LES, JESSIE, AARON, MRS. F, RICHARD, SARA, SANDRA, MARI, DEBBIE, RUBY, BRIAN, JOHN S, DAVE S, JAMES T, SOPHIA, ADAM, ROBYN, PETE, MARIAH, LOLO, B-REA, SARITA, ERIK, BRYON, NÉDA, GREG, & MY FORMER TEACHERS _at_ TRI-C & SVA. THIS BOOK HAPPENED BECAUSE _of_ YOU IN MORE WAYS THAN _you can_ KNOW SO THANK YOU.

FRIENDS

TO NYC, _my_ FIRST LOVE. YOU SHOWED ME _a way_ OF LIFE THAT I _only_ DREAMED _of_ 18 YEARS AGO _when_ I MOVED HERE. THANKS.

NYC

TO _my_ EDITOR, JUSTIN SCHWARTZ, _and_ EVERY-ONE _at_ SIMON ELEMENT.

EDITOR

TO TINA, FOR _your_ UNWAVERING SUPPORT, ENCOURAGEMENT, _and_ MAGICAL LOVE THROUGH _this_ PROCESS! _you_ ARE MY HAPPY, _my_ EVERYTHING.

T&T

TO ALL _the_ ARTISTS WHO _are_ FIGHTING _for_ MEANING, THOSE WITH _the_ MEANS WHO _are_ DOING SOMETHING MEANINGFUL, THOSE _who_ SHOW THEIR FLAWS, THOSE _who_ SHOOT & MISS FOR THE STARS & THOSE _who_ ACCEPT THEM-SELVES _for_ WHO THEY ARE: IMPERFECT HUMAN BEINGS.

ARTISTS

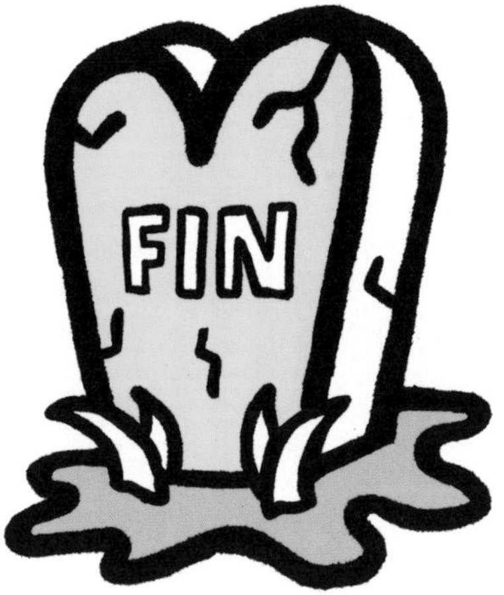
FIN

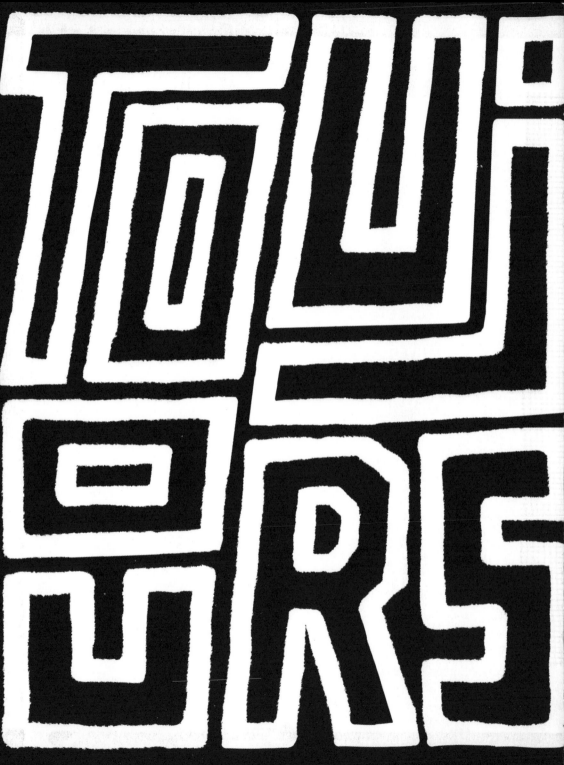